*"When they go low,
we go high."*

# WHAT'S YOUR M.O.?
by JENNIFER WORICK

## LIVE YOUR BEST LIFE,
## THE **MICHELLE OBAMA** WAY

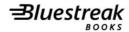

**Bluestreak**
BOOKS

Bluestreak Books is an imprint of Weldon Owen,
a Bonnier Publishing USA company
www.bonnierpublishingusa.com

Library of Congress Cataloging in Publication data is available.

ISBN: 978-1-68188-300-7

First Printed in 2018
2018 2019 2020 2021
10 9 8 7 6 5 4 3 2 1

Printed in China

Cover and interior design by
Eliza Bullock Art + Design, LLC

*What's Your M.O.?* is an unofficial book
and while every attempt has been made to determine what
Michelle Obama would do in a particular situation,
she did not directly contribute to or weigh in on the content.

# Contents

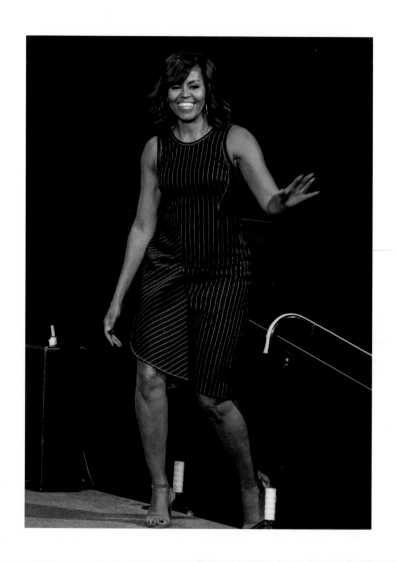

 **Introduction**

## WHAT WOULD MICHELLE OBAMA DO?
### *Let her words and actions guide the way!*

Michelle LaVaughn Robinson Obama is a *boss*. That was clear from the get-go. After graduating as salutatorian of her high school class, she went on to rule the school at Princeton and Harvard Law School. And then there was that time she was Barack's mentor when he was a summer associate at her Chicago law firm. She may not always wear pants, but she's a woman who's definitely in charge.

During her eight years as First Lady, Michelle Obama created a powerful image through example, speech, and actions. She cemented herself as a style icon and left the White House as one of the most inspiring and respected women in the world. And through her post-First Lady work and public appearances, she continues to be. So let the singular Michelle Obama guide you as you move through your own life. Be the boss you want to see in the world.

***Here's how it works:*** The book is filled with scenarios familiar to every modern woman. Whether it's juggling motherhood with a career outside the home, navigating challenging relationships, being an active citizen on a local or national level, or simply dealing with the pressures of being a woman in today's world, Michelle has been in your shoes. She gets it. The struggle is real. She came from humble beginnings on the South Side of Chicago, but a tight-knit family with rock-solid values set her on an ambitious path. Her achievements are impressive, but they didn't happen overnight or with the flick of a magic wand. This girl *worked*. And through her example, you can find practical advice and inspiration that will move you ever closer toward that elusive "best life" we all desire.

**But let's be clear:** Michelle Obama is a savvy woman who doesn't share every thought or feeling she has. In researching her life and public statements, I've extrapolated her actions and comments and applied them to scenarios that many if not all women face—in particular, working mothers. I've done my best to make educated guesses on how she would react to a situation, but I by no means can read her mind. That would probably be a federal offense.

*Go forth and make Michelle's modus operandi your own M.O.!*

*—Jennifer Worick*

# MICHELLE OBAMA'S MOST VIRAL MOMENTS

///////////////////////////////

"Evolution of Mom Dancing" sketch on *The Tonight Show with Jimmy Fallon*. Don't miss parts one (2013) and two (2015).

"Carpool Karaoke" on *The Late Late Show with James Corden*, 2016.

Greeting the Bushes on Inauguration Day at the White House, 2009.

Facial expressions during Inauguration Day, 2017. It was the face that launched a thousand memes.

Shopping at CVS with Ellen DeGeneres on *The Ellen Show*, 2016.

Surprising people who were sharing what the First Lady meant to them on *The Tonight Show with Jimmy Fallon*, 2017.

Speech after the Donald Trump *Access Hollywood* tape went public, 2016.

Speech at the Democratic National Convention, 2008.

Speech at the Democratic National Convention, 2016.

# *Family Matters*

First and foremost, *Michelle Obama*

is a mother. This "mom-in-chief" has always

been mindful of how her words and actions

can impact her daughters, as well as all

of America's youth, and she's demonstrated

how a woman can be a successful career

woman as well as a nurturing, attentive

wife and mother.

**Your schedule is increasingly busy and it's hard to find time for healthy dinners and family time.**

Michelle Obama knows all too well the importance of making the most of every moment, multitasking if necessary. She also knows that as a parent, it's her responsibility to make sure dinner is healthy. She realized this long before moving into the White House and assuming the role of First Lady. Early on, she faced the challenges of being a working mom with a lot of moving parts in the household. But after a pediatrician told her that her daughters had high body mass indices, she changed things up. No matter the appointments, homework, or extracurricular activities, the family took time to eat at home, ramping up the vegetables and saving the desserts for the weekend. As First Lady, she made it her mission to address childhood obesity in America and planted a White House garden to educate kids, set an example, and enjoy fresh seasonal produce at the dinner table.

*"I think my mother taught me what not to do. She put us first, always, sometimes to the detriment of herself. She encouraged me not to do that. She'd say being a good mother isn't all about sacrificing; it's really investing and putting yourself higher on your priority list."*

*What's Your M.O.?* When you find yourself short on time and money, consider making a soup or casserole on the weekend that you can dish up throughout the week. Cut up vegetables in advance so you can serve a simple salad or raw veggies with each meal. If you can, eat seasonally, either by picking up fresh produce at a farmer's market or joining a CSA (Community Supported Agriculture). Better yet, make eating healthy a family activity, growing your kids' favorite veggies in the backyard or a window box. They will love watching pea vines snake upwards, cherry tomatoes swell and ripen, and carrots magically appear out of the earth. Assign your kids jobs in the kitchen, teaching them how to peel potatoes or measure out ingredients. They'll quickly learn that nutritious means delicious. And you'll get some extra family time to boot.

## WAYS TO CONNECT WITH FAMILY WHEN TIME IS LIMITED

Set up a weekly phone or video call.

Create a private Facebook group for family.

Invite relatives to a Google hangout.

Start a text thread for various family members.

Plan vacations together.

Plan a family reunion every few years.

Pick a charity to collectively support. Better yet, meet for a service project like Habitat for Humanity.

Keep a family journal that everyone takes turns writing in and sending to another relative.

Start a private family blog and give everyone access to posting.

Move closer to each other or buy a vacation property together.

**Your child wants to postpone college for a year.**

Malia Obama took a gap (or bridge) year, deferring her acceptance to Harvard. Publicly, Michelle didn't say a word, but her actions spoke volumes. She supported her daughter as she took an internship with a film company in New York, encouraging her to gain skills and knowledge during her time outside the classroom. Michelle knows that experience in any form is a powerful thing and that a gap year can focus a student and provide a broader worldview.

*What's Your M.O.?* You planned and saved and expected that your child would head to a great college or university after graduating from high school. But then, curve ball! He tells you that he's going to take a gap year, traveling or interning or accumulating life experience before heading back to school. Taking a year off can be a wise decision if your kid has a plan. Many colleges will defer enrollment, so encourage him to apply to schools and secure his spot. And then ask for specifics. Is there an industry he wants to suss out? Work with him to land an internship. Does he want to travel abroad or volunteer with a nonprofit? Help him research programs and figure out how he'll pay for it. With an eye-opening year rich in experience, your child will be refreshed and ready to take on the challenges of college.

*"One of the things I realized is that if you do not take control over your time and your life, other people will gobble it up. If you don't prioritize yourself, you constantly start falling lower and lower on your list, your kids fall lower and lower on your list."*

## Your child experiences or witnesses bullying at school.

When she was 10, Michelle and her older brother Craig wondered why some kids were so mean. Their very wise parents told them that most unkindness stems from insecurity. They weren't done. The Robinsons also said that no one can make you feel bad if your values are solid and you feel good about yourself. Ultimately, it's not worth worrying what others think of you. Her parents planted the seeds of Michelle's "when they go low, we go high" philosophy. She's instilled her values in her daughters. If Malia and Sasha were to experience any form of bullying, they would shake it off and then most certainly tell their parents, as well as a teacher or principal. Sasha and Malia no doubt will continue to speak up and speak out, using their unique position as first daughters to decry cruel words and actions.

> *"My girls are the first thing I think about when I wake up in the morning and the last thing I think about when I go to bed. When people ask me how I'm doing, I say, 'I'm only as good as my most sad child.'"*

*"I want my girls to really be free, to reach and dream for whatever they can imagine. I don't want anybody telling them what they can't do. I want them to be proud to live in this country. I want them to be able to travel the world with pride. And I don't want that just for my girls. I want that for all of our children, and we're not there. We're not there."*

**What's Your M.O.?** You want to protect your kids, and sometimes you might think it's best not to make waves. That's understandable. There can be consequences to doing the right thing, such as becoming the focus of increased bullying or jeers by classmates. Kids can be downright ruthless and often wield social media as a weapon. Even if they aren't being personally mistreated, your children may have seen a classmate being picked on, another kid who has a mother with feelings as fierce as yours. Encourage your kids to tell you whenever they see or experience something unkind. Go with them and talk to the school or the bully's parents together. Set an example, showing them how to stand up for what you believe is right, even if it means confronting someone and calling them out. In Michelle's eyes, a rocky childhood is an asset that prepares a person for life. Resilience is born out of often-challenging experiences. Help your kids realize that bullying is just a bump on what is hopefully a very long and rewarding road.

*"With every word we utter, with every action we take, we know our kids are watching us. We as parents are their most important role models. And let me tell you, Barack and I take that same approach to our jobs as President and First Lady because we know that our words and actions matter, not just to our girls, but to children across this country, kids who tell us, 'I saw you on TV, I wrote a report on you for school.'"*

**Your kids complain about their challenges, be it homework, chores, their appearance, fill in the blank.**

As self-described mom-in-chief, Michelle knows that she is her daughters' mother, not always their best friend. It is her job to instill values and good habits, help them be physically healthy and safe. While they have incredibly privileged lives, Michelle expects them to appreciate the less fortunate. When Malia brought up the challenges of life in the White House, Michelle had none of it. "You want to see hardship? You want to see struggle? You don't have it, kid." Both she and Barack wanted their kids to take minimum-wage jobs as teens—Sasha worked the register at a seafood restaurant on Martha's Vineyard. As fortunate as their lives are, her daughters were still expected to clean their rooms and do their homework, learning life skills and gaining perspective that will help them as they set out on their own.

*What's Your M.O.?* You probably aren't living in the White House with a Secret Service detail, but you and your kids have your own set of challenges. The trick is not to solve your kids' problems but to give them tools and skills so they can solve them on their own. If your kids repeatedly complain about something, ask them what they can do to change the situation. If it's too much homework, for instance, ask them how they might be able to schedule their after-school time differently or break down their homework into doable pieces. And they may roll their eyes, but give examples of how fortunate they are in comparison to kids in underserved communities or other countries. Even taking them for a day of volunteer work in the community can help put things in better perspective. And finally, urge them to ask for help—from you, from teachers, from classmates, from anyone who can offer them a hand up.

**Money's tight in the household, but you still want to find a way to spend fun quality time with your family.**

When Michelle was growing up, her family was on a budget. Her father, Fraser, took the family on Sunday drives, using it as an adventure and educational experience. The Robinsons discovered new areas around Chicago and engaged in rich conversations, often sparked by Fraser's deep well of knowledge and stories. Both Michelle and her brother Craig remember those drives as instrumental in developing a broader worldview beyond their corner of the world.

*What's Your M.O.?* Take a cue from the Robinson family. Get in the car and drive. Drive around your neighborhood, plan a weekend or summer road trip, and create a regular ritual that the whole family can participate in and look forward to. Let each family member take a turn picking a direction or destination or topic of conversation. In addition to sharing stories or answering questions your kids may have, add some learning games such as quizzing your kids on state or country capitals. And cars aren't the only mode of transportation or opportunity for conversation and discovery. If you live in a large city, jump on a train or bus. Invest in bikes for the whole family and exercise together while discovering new routes. Don't discount the simple pleasure of an after-dinner walk through the neighborhood. It has the added benefit of helping the whole family (and maybe dog) get some extra steps in.

*"Remember who you always were, where you came from, who your parents were, how they raised you. Because that authentic self is going to follow you all through life, so make sure that it's solid so it's something that you can hold on and be proud of for the rest of your life."*

"I remember his compassion. I remember the words, his advice, the way he lived life, and I am trying each and every day to apply that to how I raise my kids. I want his legacy to live through them."

## You are sending your kids to a new school.

As mom-in-chief, Michelle made it clear that her primary role was as a mother. So when the Obamas moved into the White House, she toured D.C. schools, settling on Sidwell Friends, a private school that former first kids like Chelsea Clinton had attended. With a Secret Service detail and classmates from wealthy, privileged backgrounds, Malia and Sasha weren't in Kansas (or Chicago) any more. Michelle worked hard to develop routines, encouraging her daughters to hang out with their friends and go to camp and get involved in school activities. And they continued their tradition of family dinners, giving Michelle and Barack a chance to hear what was going on in their daughters' lives and reconnect on a daily basis.

***What's Your M.O.?*** Sending your children off to a new school is hard, no matter what the situation. Make yourself more available than usual for the first week or two. Meet their teachers. Ask questions, certainly, about your kids' day, classmates, and teachers. But also just listen. Give them room to open up and tell you what they like and think and feel. You'll learn more by letting them take the lead.

*"I am an example of what is possible when girls*
*from the very beginning of their lives*
*are loved and nurtured by people around them."*

# Good Relations

Communication and connection are hallmarks

of *Michelle Obama's* personality.

Learn from the master how to cultivate

meaningful relationships.

**Your partner has a hectic job and you find yourself shouldering most of the household responsibilities.**

During Barack's early years in elected office, Michelle wasn't exactly thrilled to be a single parent much of the week while Barack commuted or stayed in Springfield and then Washington. While on the campaign trail, he was absent again as he criss-crossed the state and then the country. She herself had a soaring, meaningful career but also had her hands full as the mother of two active young daughters. She even brought Sasha to a job interview (which she nailed).

*"When I first met him, I fell in deep like."*

But she had to admit that she couldn't do it all, or do it perfectly. Michelle relied heavily on family and friends, arranged her job hours around her kids' schedule, and did her best to be present for dinner and bedtime. But communication is key: Michelle dropped some truth on her husband, who became very aware of the lopsided parenting and lopsided career trajectories caused by his absence. Once in the White House, he was actually able to spend more quality time—such as dinners—with his family since he was grounded in one primary location.

**What's Your M.O.?** You do what you can, you do what you have to. Cut corners about things that don't matter (it's okay if the windowsills are dusty for another week) and focus on the things that give meaning to your life. It could be your children, your aging parents, your pets, your career, adventure travel, restoring an old home. Once you fix on what's important, make a list of what's really not all that critical and work on letting it go. Most importantly, communicate with your partner. Work together to find ways for both of you to stay engaged in your home and family. Can your partner take over bedtime duties so there's special time carved out each day with the children? Maybe the two of you can menu plan, shop, and cook on the weekend for next week's meals. Think about how to integrate your partner into the household, playing to both of your strengths if possible. It's not going to be ideal or perfectly balanced, but the important thing is that you're feeling heard and finding ways to keep moving your own dreams and goals forward.

*"The big thing I figured out was that I was pushing to make Barack be something I wanted him to be for me. I believed that if only he were around more often, everything would be better. So I was depending on him to make me happy. Except it didn't have anything to do with him. I needed support. I didn't necessarily need it from Barack."*

## You're having a hard time finding alone time and keeping the romance alive.

It's a challenge to keep the flame burning, even in the best circumstances. As a power couple, Michelle and Barack have to be more mindful than most to not take their relationship for granted. One of the first outings the First Couple had upon entering the White House was a date night with dinner and a Broadway show in New York. Critics wailed about the expense, but the president stood firm. He had promised his wife. But it's the small moments in between the big events that provide the glue. In a quiet moment after the 2009 inaugural ball, there's a beautiful photo of Michelle and Barack touching foreheads while she is draped in his suit jacket over her gown. That one photo speaks volumes about their relationship and connection, forged out of mutual respect and consideration.

*"Barack is one of the few men I've met who is not intimidated by strong women. He relishes the fact that I'm not impressed by him."*

> *"Our life before moving to Washington was filled with simple joys. Saturdays at soccer games, Sundays at Grandma's house. And a date night for Barack and me was either dinner or a movie, because as an exhausted mom, I couldn't stay awake for both."*

**What's Your M.O.?** Don't worry about jetting off to a romantic weekend on a tropical island. Romance can bloom on the home front. Spend an extra five minutes in bed in the morning or at night talking about the day or whatever's on your mind, hold hands and find ways to touch each other (an impromptu shoulder massage is always appreciated), take a bath together, leave a note in a suitcase before a business trip. Small gestures and consideration will keep your relationship on solid ground even with the most hectic of schedules.

**Your friend is dragging you down with her constant negativity and you're considering ghosting her.**

There are no friends or family in Michelle's life who view the glass as half empty. Her family taught her to work hard, achieve, and not make excuses. Her father, who was afflicted with multiple sclerosis, worked for the water plant until he passed away at 55. Despite his deteriorating condition, he rarely missed a day of work. Her college friends, many of whom came from challenging backgrounds, went on to impressive careers. These are all optimists at heart, people who strive. When she was heading up Public Allies, an organization that provided training and public service apprenticeships, she routinely met with ambitious youth from housing projects and lower-income neighborhoods who often had troubled backgrounds, including being expelled from school and hanging out with a rough crowd. She didn't mince words, telling them to get it together and start thinking of good colleges. Keep your eye on the prize, think of your future. She was always supportive and encouraging, but she didn't shy away from calling out excuses and bad behavior.

*What's Your M.O.?* Sure, bad things happen to good people. Life isn't fair. But if you have a friend who'd rather sit around and complain than take steps to move her life forward, it's time for you to take action by either having a kind but candid conversation or backing away. These people will pull focus, sap your energy, and frustrate you. You can see their potential, but they can't or won't see it. Complacency is not your jam, but it may be theirs. Before quitting the friendship entirely, consider whether it's worth it to have a heartfelt conversation with her, particularly if she is a longtime friend. With kindness, remind her that how she's living her life today is how she lives her life. Does she want to spend her days wallowing or complaining, or would she like to create a meaningful life and work toward becoming her best self? If your honesty doesn't move the needle, it may be time to call it quits and seek out more aspirational people to spend time with. It's not your job to help those who choose not to help themselves.

*"We should always have three friends in our lives—one who walks ahead who we look up to and follow; one who walks beside us, who is with us every step of our journey; and then, one who we reach back for and bring along after we've cleared the way."*

*"Surround yourself with goodness...
You gotta just sort of surround
yourself with people who uplift
you...You gotta find those
people because they're out there.
I tell my mentees, there's
somebody out there who loves
you and who is waiting to
love you. And you just have to find
them and that means that you
have to make room for them. And
if you're surrounded by a bunch
of lowlife folks who aren't
supporting you, then there is
no room for the people
who do love you."*

## You keep going on dates with guys who only talk about themselves.

Just like in your career, it pays to know your value when it comes to intimate relationships. Michelle didn't date extensively before Barack, not finding most men up to her standards, standards set by the example of her father and brother. She and Barack had an immediate rapport, he was deeply interested in getting to know her and her family, and she was his equal from the get-go. Michelle was equally interested in this man who had an upbringing very different from hers. If only one of them monopolized the conversation on their storied first date, they wouldn't have been able to see how their pieces fit together.

*What's Your M.O.?* While it's annoying (and far too common) to go out with people who never ask you anything about yourself, let's back up and look at your "picker." Maybe you're going out with dates who are incompatible because you're focusing on the wrong things, particularly when online dating. Get clear on what you require from a relationship and then get smarter about reading online profiles. It's far too easy to be charmed by a witty profile, flattering photo, or a flirty instant message, but take time to suss out the qualities that you value. (Maybe "understanding and loving women" is mandatory, while "being really into music" can move to the bottom of your list.) On the date, don't do that thing where you pepper him with interesting questions to draw him out and avoid awkward silences. Sit in the silence. Wait for him to reset—he may just be nervous, after all—and turn the conversation toward you. If that doesn't work, ask him what he'd like to know about you. If he continues to find ways to bring it back to himself, move on. You are far too powerful and resplendent to waste time with someone who doesn't see or appreciate you.

## You've been dating someone a long time but you suspect you deserve better.

Michelle's family used to joke about the men she dated, wondering how long they'd last before she'd find that they didn't live up to her expectations, which were high. Her brother Craig said, "We gave it a month, tops. . . . We knew he was going to do something wrong, and then it was going to be too bad for him. She held everybody to the same standard as my father, which was very high." But she wasn't being unduly picky; she knew she needed to find her match, someone who was accomplished and could hold his own. Then Barack came along and everything made sense. She liked him as a person and she felt that spark that had been missing in all her other relationships.

> *"You don't want to be with a boy who's too stupid to appreciate a smart young woman."*

*"There is nothing sexier than a smart woman . . .
we have been told to live by a certain mold;
it's time to break it."*

**What's Your M.O.?** You've been dating a perfectly nice person for a while but you're starting to wonder if you could do better and if you should cut bait. And then the other voice in your head takes over, rationalizing and saying your standards are too high and you won't find anyone better and you're being unrealistic. Just slow down! Spend some time thinking about your reservations. What is it about the relationship or person you don't like? Do you feel taken for granted, disregarded, subsumed? Does your partner have some shortcomings that just can't be overcome? When it comes right down to it, do you just not feel that certain something, that spark that tells you that you've found your "person"? After you've sat with this and separated the superficial from the significant, if your gut is telling you that this isn't the right relation-ship for you, move on. As difficult as it may be, you have to create space and time to let the right person reveal him- or herself. It will be worth the wait.

*"The men who raised me set a high bar for the type of men I'd allow into my life, which is why I went on to marry a man who had the good sense to fall in love with a woman who was his equal, and to treat me as such."*

# *Working Woman*

Let's not forget that Barack worked for *her* initially.

And that power looked good on her.

She has never diminished herself for a man or

a role. This First Lady is an equal partner

in every sense of the word.

## Your colleague asked you on a date.

Michelle initially rejected Barack's invitation, thinking it inappropriate, particularly because she was assigned to be his mentor. But, as she described it, she "fell in deep *like*." She liked pretty much everything about him and thought they could be great friends. When he pressed for a date, she resisted, even trying to set him up with her friends. But she eventually relented and they spent the day together in Chicago, visiting the Art Institute and catching a screening of *Do the Right Thing*. The rest is history. While she did enter into a relationship with a colleague, she took her time, went into it with her eyes open, and transitioned into a relationship with integrity and her professional reputation intact.

*What's Your M.O.?* Proceed with caution. Make sure you are really interested in each other before crossing the line from colleagues to romantic partners. The working world is filled with coworkers who hooked up, regretted it, and now have to work together or find new jobs. Awkward! If the chemistry and potential are real, however, spend time getting to know each other. Go slowly. Suss out what makes that person tick, what he or she cares about, and whether that jives with your own interests and values. As the relationship develops, notify your employer. Consider how you both can separate yourself on the job, perhaps by one of you being transferred to a different department. On the home front, as hard as it is, refrain from talking about the minutiae of the office—it can compromise your work life and can easily become all-consuming.

# "Know your own value."

**You want a family but don't want to sacrifice your career trajectory.**

Michelle and Barack waited a few years before jumping into parenthood. They pursued their careers, full steam ahead, until they were firmly established.

> *"People won't remember what people say about you. They will remember what you do... The best revenge is success and good work."*

Then they had Malia six years after marrying. Even then, it wasn't ideal. Barack had just been elected to the Illinois state senate and was frequently absent. Michelle, armed with an impressive resume, left her corporate law job and moved into a role at City Hall. She then worked in a variety of roles that provided immense personal and professional satisfaction and allowed for some flexibility in her daily schedule to raise her kids. But she also needed help and frequently called upon her mother, Marian, to pitch in.

*What's Your M.O.?* Navigating a career and family is a difficult decision that millions of women have and will face. We've been sold a false bill of goods that we can have it all, that whole "bring home the bacon, fry it up in a pan" baloney. No one can do it all, at least not at once. Life gets in the way, no matter how hard you try to control things and bend it to your will. Plan, yes, but then dive in and start a family. First, explore whether your partner could reduce his or her work schedule or if it makes more fiscal sense for your partner to be the stay-at-home parent. Talk to your employer about a reduced schedule or scaled-back responsibilities. If you work for yourself, outsource some projects or tasks. It's okay to take your full maternity leave, and then some. Trust that your skill set is intact. If you opt to be a stay-at-home mom for a couple of years, schedule regular calls or coffee dates with colleagues to stay top of mind and abreast of industry news. When you are ready to return to the workforce, seek out placement agencies that specialize in finding women contracts or full-time positions.

*"Work is rewarding. I love losing myself in a set of problems that have nothing to do with my husband and children. Once you've tasted that, it's hard to walk away."*

*"People can smell inauthenticity . . . In every interaction I've had with anybody who's had a connection with me, I've tried to be authentically myself. In order to do that, I learned that I have to do things I authentically care about. Because if I fundamentally deep down have a belief in the cause and it moves me, I'm gonna be excited about it. That excitement is going to be conveyed to the people I'm trying to reach. It's not gonna be a heavy lift."*

**You are torn between taking a job for the sweet salary versus pursuing a career based on passion.**

Michelle cut her salary virtually in half when she went from a corporate law firm to a job at City Hall—this while she was still saddled with student loans. But she did the math and figured out how to make her and Barack's salaries work. Never take a job for the money, her parents advised, because you'll never make enough to compensate for the pain and suffering. And the amount of experience she gained at City Hall was invaluable to her, both personally and professionally, in the long run.

*What's Your M.O.?.* Obviously, the ideal scenario would be to be paid what you're worth for a job that you love. That, unfortunately, is not always the case. There are reasons to take a well-paying salary, such as paying off loans, buying a home, or supporting a spouse and family. It might not make your pulse race or heart sing, but if it's challenging and enhances your resume and skill set in the process, go for it. It doesn't have to be forever. Create a one-, five-, and 10-year plan and map out your exit strategy so you can pivot into a job you care deeply about. Work hard, make bank, beef up your retirement and savings accounts, and move on. Nonprofit jobs and other meaningful work don't generally pay top dollar, but the tradeoff is amazing coworkers, a company with a mission, and a reason to spring out of bed with anticipation each workday. And that is worth more than the crushing despair and frustration that can come with a job you hate but don't feel you can leave. If necessary, down-sizing your lifestyle is a small price to pay for freedom from golden handcuffs.

*"I tried part time because I thought,
'I have to figure this out, I have
to be able to pick the kids up, I've got
to be able to do all this.' So I tried
part time. The only thing I found out
from part time was that you just
get paid part time. So I had vowed that
if I continued to work, that I would
never settle for part time. I knew what
my time and energy was worth."*

# You are doing the work of three people and you can't take it anymore.

Michelle knows a little something about juggling a massive workload. While at Princeton and Harvard Law School, she pushed herself to take on more. In her professional career and as a working mom and then as First Lady, she continued to assume more projects and responsibilities, pushing herself and her schedule to the limit. No woman can shoulder a massive workload without a strategy, and Michelle is no different. She carves out time to work out and mentor young people, nourishing her body and spirit. She manages her staff, leaning on them to offload some tasks that don't require her attention or expertise. She looks to her mother,

Marian, for advice and help with her daughters. To paraphrase John Donne, no woman is an island. Better yet, to quote Hillary Clinton, it takes a village . . . not only to raise a child, but to be a successful human being.

## What's Your M.O.?

If you are swamped, you have three options: get help, offload some responsibilities, or suck it up and tough it out. Help can manifest in many ways. Take on an intern. Prioritize projects with your manager, staggering deadlines so you can focus on one thing at a time. Request funds for a short-term contractor to assist on one particular project; better yet, hire them as project manager and let them drive the work under your supervision. Reassigning some responsibilities altogether is tricky, as employers often view this as a downsizing of your job description, even though you are basically doing the work of three employees and rocking several job descriptions. Create a list of your current responsibilities and projects, and highlight those that leverage your unique skill set and work with your manager to reassign the tasks that are below your pay grade and accruing extra expense because you are doing them. If you can handle the work and are willing to forgo personal time, ask to be fairly compensated so the resentment/victimization subsides. Come up with a sum, bonus, or promotion that you deserve before you start the conversation.

*"Your success will be determined by your own confidence and fortitude."*

## You feel as if you're being passed over and not getting your due at the office.

From her early school days, Michelle's approach has always been to study harder, work harder, fight harder, and overachieve. Most of the time that pays off, but occasionally even she struggles to be acknowledged for her work. As a senior at Princeton, Michelle was gobsmacked when a professor told her, "You're not the hottest thing I've seen coming out of the gate." Who says that, especially to a student who had aced his class? She never made excuses or cried foul (although she had to be both hurt and angry initially). She worked her butt off and leaned in, working as his research assistant. "I knew that it was my responsibility to show my professor how wrong he was about me." Show him she did—he offered to write her a letter of recommendation.

*What's Your M.O.?* Look at your own performance and attitude and identify areas where you can improve. Talk to your manager and ask for her honest evaluation on things you can do to exceed expectations, and then agree to a time when the two of you will revisit the issue of a promotion or raise, say in three or six months. If you are already rocking your job, raise your profile: participate in your company's interest/affinity groups or initiatives such as the annual giving campaign, join the board of a local nonprofit, or mentor new hires. But as a woman, you know that inequality exists, and life and the workplace aren't always fair. If you have outperformed your coworkers and your own job description and still aren't recognized for your efforts, speak up. Schedule a meeting with your manager, laying out your case for promotion, using concrete examples of your exceptional work. Talk about how you contributed to the bottom line, how you made or saved money for the company. If that doesn't move the needle, consider taking your case (again, with specific details about your contribution, industry salary statistics, your annual reviews and advancement in relation to the rest of the company, etc.) to a higher-up or human resources. If you still feel unsupported and unrecognized, seek a new gig with a company that advocates for parity and equity.

*"I think my generation of professional women are sort of waking up and realizing that we potentially may not be able to have it all, not at the same time."*

"As women and young girls, we have to invest that time in getting to understand who we are and liking who we are. Because I like me. I've liked me for a very long time . . . But you gotta work to get to that place. And if you're going out into the world as a professional and you don't know who you are, you don't know what you want, you don't know how much you're worth, then you have to be brave."

# *Style + Substance*

*Michelle Obama* redefined not only

the role of First Lady but the style as well.

Mixing J.Crew with Jason Wu,

her style evolution has been a thing

to behold—and *emulate*.

"What I owe the American people is to let them see who I am so there are no surprises. I don't want to be anyone but Michelle Obama. And I want people to know what they're getting."

**You want to create a consistent image to promote your personal brand.**

Long before she became First Lady, Michelle was an accomplished attorney and hospital executive. Her spouse was an up-and-coming political figure. In the interests of time and personal image, she needed to lock down her style and minimize shopping time. She turned to Ikram Goldman, the owner of Chicago's chic Ikram boutique, for what would develop into a dream collaboration. Goldman acted as personal shopper, stylist, and intermediary, commissioning garments from favorite designers for important events.

*What's Your M.O.?* While you may not be casting about for an Inaugural Ball gown, it still makes style sense to enlist the help of a pro. Work with a stylist or develop a relationship with the owner of your favorite local boutique. Use the often-free personal shopper service at department stores. They can scout looks for you, set items aside, and even arrange for alterations or customized looks. Work with your team to translate the season's trends for your personal brand. The trick is to not go rogue and buy that prairie dress when you've been cultivating an edgy image with a closet full of minimalist garments.

*"We take our bangs and we stand in front of important things that the world needs to see. And eventually, people stop looking at the bangs and they start looking at what we're standing in front of."*

ON THE MEDIA ATTENTION OVER HER NEW BANGS AND HOW FIRST LADIES HANDLE SCRUTINY

# 10 MOMENTS WHERE MICHELLE SLAYED

//////////////////////////////////

**Appearance on *The View*, June 2008:** Her $148 black-and-white printed dress came from White House Black Market and quickly sold out nationwide.

**Election night victory dress, November 2008:** Her red-and-black Narciso Rodriguez sparkling dress offered a fresh take on color blocking.

**Inauguration day, January 2009:** In an Isabel Toledo lemongrass-hued dress and lace jacket, paired with green J.Crew leather gloves, she managed to look chic, ladylike, and thoroughly modern.

**Her first Inaugural Ball, January 2009:** In an ivory one-shoulder Jason Wu confection, she looked like a literal breath of fresh air.

**Hula hooping on the South Lawn, October 2009:** For a White House fitness event, she wore one of her many bright cardigans cinched by a thick studded belt. To complete the casual but polished look, she added slim black Capri pants and flats, which she kicked off as she ran across the lawn.

**Her first official White House portrait, 2009:** As she stood beneath a portrait of Thomas Jefferson in a black sleeveless sheath and pearls, she looked timeless and contemporary.

**Meeting Queen Elizabeth, April 2009:** She wore a black-and-white Jason Wu satin dress in a classic silhouette but created a buzz when she topped it with a snug black cardigan. Even the Queen can't rein in Michelle's love of a cardi.

**Democratic National Convention speech, July 2016:** Michelle looked like Democratic party royalty in a simple royal blue Christian Siriano dress when she delivered an impassioned, savvy speech at the convention.

**The Obamas' final state dinner, October 2016:** The First Lady wore a Versace gown that looked like liquid metal in a rose gold color that draped over her in the most delicious way. She looked hot *and* regal.

**French Polynesia, April 2017:** When a photo surfaced of Michelle rocking her natural hair, African Americans rejoiced on Twitter.

## You love a part of your body but don't know if it's appropriate to highlight it at the office.

Welcome to the gun show! Michelle Obama has killer arms and she's not afraid to show them. In fact, her first White House portrait shows her exuding confidence in a bare-shouldered black sheath and pearls. She showcased her well-earned asset and kept it classy and appropriate. Women have been wearing sleeveless dresses to work and special occasions for decades, but somehow, critics decried that she was pushing the envelope a bit too far. She held her ground and continued baring her arms in photo shoots, at President Obama's first State of the Union address, you name it. She understands her body and how to dress it. She also takes into account the occasion and has found a way to highlight her assets while always dressing appropriately.

*What's Your M.O.?* There will always be haters. Don't listen to them. If you have a feature and want to show it, figure out which cuts and styles of clothing are most flattering. That said, consider your work environment. If you work in a conservative office, a skirt slit up to there is not the ideal way to highlight toned legs. Rather, a slim pencil skirt or skinny trousers will do the trick. If you work in a more creative environment, you can probably get away with a miniskirt, but pair it with dark or colorful tights rather than bare legs. You want colleagues to notice, not ogle, you.

"So my first reaction isn't 'Who made this?'
But 'Let's try it on. What does it look
like? Oooh, that's cute. Oh, wow. I never
thought of wearing something like this.
Let's put a belt on it. I feel gooood in this.'
There are definitely designers that I
love, people I love to work with. And who
they are as people matters. Are they
good people? Do they treat their staff well?
Do they treat my staff well? Are they
young? Can I give them a boost? But! When
all of that is equal . . . is it cute?!"

## You need to be comfortable but still stylish.

During her time as First Lady, Michelle got flak for wearing shorts and going barefoot, but she didn't sweat it. She wore—gasp!—a cardigan to meet the queen. She slips into flats and kitten heels with regularity. While on vacation in French Polynesia in 2017, she let her hair revert to its natural wave, putting it back in a polka-dotted headband. Michelle always opts for comfort and has proven that comfort and style aren't mutually exclusive.

***What's Your M.O.?*** Wear what you love, and always reach for favorite pieces. If you wear what feels good, you are more likely to be relaxed and focused on the event or task at hand. Think about the event you're attending. If you're doing something sporty, dress for function. If you are going to a cocktail party and will be standing for a good two hours, you might want to swap the stiletto for a lower heel. Curate a closet of well-fitting clothes in flattering colors. Don't be a label whore; Michelle has proven that you can mix high and low brands to create a style that's entirely your own. And never forget the power of accessorizing: zhush up the most basic sweater or dress with a well-placed brooch or statement necklace.

## *"I can be comfortable in anything."*

## You have a closet full of clothes but can't seem to find anything to wear.

Michelle Obama has a drool-worthy wardrobe, full of designer labels and one-of-a-kind designs. It wouldn't have been a surprise to anyone if she wore something completely different for every outing. But she didn't. She reached for what she loved, which included J.Crew cardigans, kitten heels, and wide belts. Girl loves her belts. In fact, Barack called one favorite thick metallic belt her *Star Trek* belt. It's easy to see what clothes Michelle loves and feels comfortable in—it shows on her face and in her body language, as it does for many women. She has a confidence and ease that will be absent when your feet are killing you or you're wearing something that is outside your style comfort zone.

*What's Your M.O.?* Take a nod from Michelle and Marie Kondo, author of *The Life-Changing Magic of Tidying Up*. Pull out all of your clothes and put them on a clothing rack or on the bed. Try everything on and keep only the items that feel great, are flattering, and "spark joy." Once you've culled your wardrobe, experiment with different outfits and take selfies in all of the winners. You'll always have a closet of slammin' looks at the ready.

"First and foremost, I wear what I love. That's what women have to focus on: what makes them happy and what makes them feel comfortable and beautiful. If I can have any impact, I want women to feel good about themselves and have fun with fashion."

## You have loads of style but your partner doesn't and shows no interest in developing any.

As Michelle tells it, when she met Barack, he wasn't exactly a fashion plate, wearing "cruddy" suits and too-small shoes. He has the good fortune to be tall and lean, which makes clothes hang well on him, which made him look decidedly more stylish as he entered public office. But even then, he opted for comfy dad jeans instead of something more on trend. For the most part, Michelle lets Barack be Barack and in return, he lets her do her. She knows that fashion has its place but that it isn't everything. Barack may not be a sartorial savant, but he has rock-solid values and puts his energies toward public service and worthwhile causes. In the face of that, who cares about a tired pair of pleated khakis?

> *"Barack and I—as partners, as friends, as lovers—we accessorize each other in many ways. The best thing I love having on me is Barack on my arm and vice versa."*

**What's Your M.O.?** Your partner may not dress up to your standards, but consider this: Maybe his lack of style *is* his style. That said, there are little things you can do to spruce up your partner's wardrobe. Ask questions about favorite clothing: Why is she so drawn to graphic tees? How come he can't part with that ratty pair of jeans or pointy blue Italian loafers (what was bought in Vegas should stay in Vegas)? Armed with this feedback, try shopping for a garment or two, and see how it goes. Do not bring home bags full of clothing because you're bound to be disappointed. But perhaps a pair

> *"Barack puts on his suit and tie and he's out the door. I'm getting my hair and makeup done. The kids, I've got to brush their hair. And he's always saying, 'Where are you? Where are you going?'"*

of perfectly fitted jeans will blow his mind or the feel of a cashmere sweater will make her consider the benefits of well-chosen, luxe items. When you clean out your closet, suggest making it a family affair and weed out all closets, first pulling out ancient, stained, or damaged items. If that goes well, prune further and slowly replace with more flattering items that will make both of you happy.

> *"Put a little pin on [the dress] and you've got something going on."*

 **You have a wardrobe full of flattering, well-fitting basics but it lacks style and flair.**

Michelle Obama is no stranger to suits, dresses, and work separates. They all fit her like a glove and provide a great foundation and canvas for her to add color, sparkle, and texture. No matter how classic the garment is, she always manages to elevate it with a personal touch. She regularly pins a sparkly vintage brooch to her dress or blouse, she adds multiple strands of pearls or bold necklaces to solid-colored sheaths, and she loves herself a wide belt to add shape and interest to the most casual of outfits. Layering is another secret to Michelle's signature style. She slips colorful cardigans on over dresses, even opting for a snug black sweater over a satin gown to meet Queen Elizabeth.

***What's Your M.O.?*** It's not rocket science but it does take some time to build a collection of bold accessories and some ingenuity to wear them in creative ways. The good news is that you've already done the heavy lifting, building a wardrobe of go-to garments. Now the fun can begin. Seriously. If you have any heirloom jewelry, shine it up and put it into rotation. Stay abreast of trends in different ways. Thumb through catalogs and online sites, talk to your favorite salespeople, find and follow a fashion blog by a writer whose style you admire and that seems attainable. Join a monthly subscription service that will send you new accessories to own or borrow for a small monthly fee. Look beyond jewelry to scarves, gloves, handbags, and shoes. A killer handbag or unique menswear wingtip oxford will always pull focus and garner admiring (i.e. envious) glances. Michelle says she wears what she loves, and so should you. In your travels, seek out special items that you are eager to work into your wardrobe.

*"We ladies know J.Crew. You can get some good stuff online... When you don't have time, you've gotta click. Click on!"*

Every time you reach for that quartz ring or wool scarf, you'll think about your adventures. Getting dressed will become a treat, rather than a mindless task.

# *Strength* *in the* *face of* *Adversity*

During her time in the White House, the *First Lady*

witnessed many national tragedies. Through it

all, she displayed grace and compassion.

Learn how to navigate a difficult situation

through the example she set.

## You are trying to be strong for friends and family but you are overwhelmed.

If you think you're overwhelmed by a busy schedule or life in general, try relocating your family to a new city, getting your kids enrolled in a new school, hiring a huge household staff, and assuming a highly scheduled calendar of events and meetings, all while under the scrutiny of a nation. No sweat, right? Ha! Michelle Obama makes things look easy, with her presence and poise, but moving into the White House could bring the strongest woman to her knees. The First Lady called in reinforcements. Her close friends from Chicago visited frequently, she recharged away from the public eye at Camp David, and she persuaded her mother to move into the White House. Marian helped out with Malia and Sasha and, perhaps more importantly, offered support and advice to her daughter. There's no better sounding board than a loving and candid mother.

*What's Your M.O.?* Reach out. Surround yourself with loved ones. Think about the oxygen mask instructions you are given before a flight: take care of yourself before assisting others. After all, you are no good to loved ones if you are operating on a low battery. And the best way to do that is to show some vulnerability and ask for support. There's no shame in your game if you admit you need help, be it on a professional or personal front. Ask your neighbor if he'll walk your dog, reach out to a friend for help retooling your website or social media presence, ask your mom for a loan. There are many people in your life who love you and will be happy to help, not judge. Women have been sold a false bill of goods—we can't do it all, not at one time, and not without help.

"When I'm unhappy with something, people know, because I don't want to hold on to it. I'd rather deal immediately with the stuff that bothers me, so using my network—my girlfriends, my husband, my mom—I talk a lot, I vent. Even if there are no answers, sharing the emotions helps keep me stable."

"What message are our little girls
hearing about who they should look like, how
they should act? What lessons are they
learning about their value as professionals,
as human beings, about their dreams
and aspirations? And how is this affecting
men and boys in this country?
Because I can tell you that the men in
my life do not talk about women like this.
And I know that my family is not
unusual. And to dismiss this as everyday
locker-room talk is an insult to decent
men everywhere...Strong men—men who
are truly role models—don't need to
put down women to make themselves feel
powerful. People who are truly strong
lift others up. People who are truly powerful
bring others together."

FROM A SPEECH GIVEN SHORTLY AFTER DONALD TRUMP'S
ACCESS HOLLYWOOD VIDEO WENT PUBLIC

## You experience or witness sexual harassment.

As women, we cannot tolerate sexual harassment in the workplace or anywhere else, whether it happens to us personally or to a fellow female. Michelle has repeatedly advocated for women and spoken out against men who harass women. "Strong men—men who are truly role models—don't need to put down women to make themselves feel powerful. People who are truly strong lift others up." So said Michelle after Donald Trump's *Access Hollywood* video went public. She also said that the video shook her to her core. It should unsettle us all to hear men talk so disparagingly about women. Sadly, we've probably all experienced some form of verbal or physical harassment during our life. But that doesn't mean that we should accept it.

*What's Your M.O.?* Some women are afraid to speak up for fear of retribution or job loss. That's understandable. By staying silent, however, we perpetuate the problem. Speak up. If this happens in the workplace, report the incident to HR. If you experience verbal abuse online, report it to the social network or website and maybe even to the harasser's friends, family, or employer. Harassed socially? You guessed it: report it. It's important to create a record of harassment for own protection. We have to stand up to bullying, which is what harassment is, not only for ourselves but for the young women who come after us. And remember: not only is it not okay, it's illegal.

## After spending months or years on a project you care deeply about, the powers that be kill it.

Months after he took office, it was announced that President Trump would end Let Girls Learn, an initiative Michelle spearheaded that would facilitate educational opportunities to tens of millions of girls around the world. He also loosened the guidelines and standards for healthy school lunches that Michelle fought to put in place nationwide. Two steps forward, one step back. Michelle has encountered setbacks before. And her reaction has always been to dig in harder. She will continue to speak out and work to advance educational opportunities and better nutrition for kids in America and abroad. She has built up a reputation for integrity, heart, and determination and while she is no longer First Lady, she still has enormous influence and leverage to move the needle forward.

> *"You see, our glorious diversity—our diversity of faiths, and colors and creeds—that is not a threat to who we are. It **makes us** who we are."*

***What's Your M.O.?*** First of all, let yourself be disappointed. Having meaningful work torpedoed or dismissed is demoralizing and heartbreaking. But the fight for change is long and ongoing. If your project was killed, find out why. Armed with information, try to find a solution. If budget is the issue, can it be streamlined? If the company has changed focus, can the project be retooled to align with the new direction? Can it be taken elsewhere or funded by donors or a grant? Think around the problem and don't give up on something you believe in.

# 10 INSTANT WAYS TO LIFT YOUR SPIRIT

/////////////////////////////

**Take a walk in the woods.**
The First Lady escaped to Camp David when she wanted some room to breathe and recharge. There's something magical about a simple walk in nature.

**Dance like no one's watching.**
Michelle likes to dance, even if someone is watching, as evidenced by her Let's Move! initiative and two appearances on *The Tonight Show with Jimmy Fallon* demonstrating the history of mom dancing.

**Walk the dog.** One of Michelle's favorite breaks is to walk Bo and Sunny. After leaving the White House, she tweeted a photo of them while taking a sidewalk stroll.

**Garden.** Michelle not only planned the White House kitchen garden, she spent time in it, planting, weeding, and harvesting its bounty.

**Drive.** Michelle lamented the fact that she wasn't able to drive while First Lady. It's something she's enjoyed since she was a kid and her dad took the family on Sunday drives.

**Perform a random act of kindness.**
Paying for a stranger's coffee or giving someone a hug—Michelle Obama's signature gesture—cheers you as well as others.

**Sing your favorite song at the top of your lungs**. When she rocked out to Stevie Wonder in a *Carpool Karaoke* segment, the First Lady's joy was on full display.

**Plan a trip.** Despite public criticism, Michelle planned various trips with her family during their years in the White House, seeing travel as an important cultural experience and much-needed break.

**Reread your favorite book.** Some of Michelle's favorite books include *Song of Solomon* by Toni Morrison, *Life of Pi* by Yann Martel, and *Where the Wild Things Are* by Maurice Sendak (revisiting childhood favorites is always uplifting).

**Meditate for five minutes.** As Michelle puts it, "There are just some times you have to give yourself space to be quiet."

## Your world was just shaken by tragedy.

A close college friend lost her fight with cancer, and shortly thereafter, Michelle's beloved father, Fraser, passed away at the age of 55 after struggling with multiple sclerosis. Just 27, Michelle was devastated. In her grief, she questioned her career path. She was making a handsome salary as an up-and-coming corporate attorney but didn't feel like she was making a difference. "I began to do a little soul searching. I began to ask myself some hard questions. Questions like, 'If I die tomorrow, what did I really do with my life? What kind of a mark would I leave? How would I be remembered?' And none of my answers satisfied me." Shortly thereafter, she took a public service job at Chicago City Hall, working for Mayor Richard M. Daley. That set her on a course of a variety of positions that helped the community and, most notably, its kids. Speaking of kids, she and Barack were shaken by the shooting death of Hadiya Pendelton, a 15-year-old honor student who, like Michelle, was from the South Side of Chicago. Two years later, Michelle delivered a commencement address to King College Prep High School, urging Hadiya's classmates to take their collective tragedy and go forward in the world with determination and joy. Michelle knows from experience that pain and hardship can eventually give way to strength of character and resolve.

**What's Your M.O.?** If you experience a tragic event in your life, perhaps the death of a loved one or an unexpected medical diagnosis, use it as an opportunity to take stock of your life. Question your path in life. Are you living your values? Are you proud of the work you do? Are you satisfied with how you spend your days? List all the things, large and small, that you are not completely satisfied with, be it career, travel, family time, artistic aspirations, fitness, etc. Then, make another list about how you can start making small changes right this minute to become your best self. Whether it's taking flying lessons, switching careers, running for office, becoming more active in your church or community, or carving out more time for family, you can be on your way to deeper personal satisfaction in short order. Don't wait for the next tragedy to remind you that you have one life to live with meaning and purpose.

*"That is the story of this country, the story that has brought me to this stage tonight, the story of generations of people who felt the lash of bondage, the shame of servitude, the sting of segregation, but who kept on striving and hoping and doing what needed to be done so that today I wake up every morning in a house that was built by slaves."*

**You revealed something personal on social media and you are now being trolled.**

No one can make you feel bad about yourself if you have inner confidence and believe in yourself. This was a lesson Marian and Fraser Robinson instilled in their daughter and boy, has it come in handy. The First Lady has endured more than her fair share of slings and arrows, from critiques of her clothing choices and appearance to more ugly and racist comments. Much of this has occurred on the internet, as haters spew their comments behind a veil of anonymity. But thanks to the lessons she learned as a young black girl growing up on the South Side of Chicago, she doesn't let negative remarks get under her skin. As she said, "You can't be reading all that stuff. I mean, that's like letting somebody come up and slap you." You wouldn't accept that kind of behavior in the real world, and there's no reason you should allow that sort of abuse online.

> *"If I wilted every time somebody in my life mischaracterized me or called me a bad name, I would have never finished Princeton, would have never gone to Harvard, and wouldn't be sitting here with him. So these are the lessons we want to teach our kids. You know who you are, so what anybody else says is just interesting fodder."*

**What's Your M.O.?** Online comments can be unsettling and down-right scary. Every day, someone is trolled or "doxxed" (meaning their personal information such as phone number and address is publicly posted) online, ruthlessly and relentlessly mocked and threatened by one or thousands of faceless online users. Unlike the First Lady, you don't have the Secret Service to protect you, so you have to take care of your own personal security. If you do see something that causes your Spidey sense to kick in, heed your instinct and report the comment to the social network and, if truly threatening, to the authorities as well. While it's natural to want to fire off a rage-filled response, resist. It only escalates the situation and elevates your blood pressure. Take a cue from Michelle and tune out the haters (who probably hate themselves most of all) as best you can. In fact, step away from social media altogether now and again. Unplugging can reset your internal confidence and self-assurance so you can go out into the world and fight in battles that actually matter.

> *"One of the lessons that I grew up with was to always stay true to yourself and never let what somebody else says distract you from your goals. And so when I hear about negative and false attacks, I really don't invest any energy in them, because I know who I am."*

# You're starting over in a new place and you don't know how to rebuild your life.

Michelle knows a thing or two about moving to a new city and taking on a new role for herself. When she was asked what she was going to do as First Lady, she said, "I have to wait until I get there to figure out what that's going to feel like for me." She allowed herself time to get settled. She took into account the role and circumstances, as well as her own passions and interests, before she defined the position for herself. That said, she wasn't starting from scratch, and neither are you. Building on her career, experience, and interests, she brought a whole lot to the table, and all of that rich personal history guided her to create initiatives around childhood obesity, education for girls around the world, and mental health awareness and assistance for veterans, while never forgetting her primary role as "mom-in-chief." And now she's starting another new chapter in her life. After leaving the White House, she and Barack took some much needed time off and then jumped back into their work. Wasting no time, she inked a publishing deal for her memoir and started making public appearances, talking about issues close to her heart. She and Barack are shaping the Barack Obama Presidential Center in Chicago. A new location is an opportunity to grow in ways you never imagined.

> *"Instead of letting your hardships and failures discourage or exhaust you, let them inspire you. Let them make you even hungrier to succeed."*

**What's Your M.O.?** Starting over can be painful. But it's also an opportunity for growth and positive change. Divorce, moving back home to care for an ailing parent, recovering from a disease, bouncing back after bankruptcy—life continues to throw us detours and we often find ourselves far off the carefully mapped-out path we planned for ourselves. But you're not lost. You bring with you all the life experience you've accumulated, as well as friends, skills, and experience. The first thing you need to do is shore up your community—reach out to any acquaintances you know in town. That's a start. Then turn your attention to community events, places of worship, coffee shops, anywhere you can make meaningful connections. Next, look at your living situation and determine what will make it feel more like home to you. Hang favorite pieces of art, put out sentimental items, paint the walls a cheery color. Last, use this fresh start as a chance to get to know yourself better. What do you want to leave behind and shed from your old life? Now's your opportunity to redefine who you want to be in the world. And that's about as exciting as it gets.

*"Barack and I were raised with so many of the same values: that you work hard for what you want in life; that your word is your bond and you do what you say you're going to do; that you treat people with dignity and respect, even if you don't know them, and even if you don't agree with them."*

# *Education Nation*

*Michelle* understands the power and value

of education in all its forms and has

consistently emphasized the role education

plays, during the most formative years

and throughout one's life.

> *"If I point to anything that makes me who I am, it's that I have a whole lot of common sense. I've got a good mind and a good ability to read people and situations."*

 **You are smarter than the average bear but your education and intelligence make you appear arrogant and off-putting.**

The campaign trail can be grueling and unforgiving. When Barack began his campaign for president in late 2006, it quickly became apparent that Michelle was his biggest asset. She listened, asked questions, studied up, and delivered powerful, authentic speeches about her husband and America's future. In one speech, she said, "For the first time in my adult life, I am proud of my country." She was raked over the coals, with conservatives lambasting her for talking ill of a country where she graduated from two Ivy League schools, made a considerable salary, and was basically living the dream. Of course, her comments were taken out of context, but it didn't matter. She had an uphill battle to dispel perceptions of her as arrogant and strident. But over time, she did just that, connecting with Americans of all economic and education levels by sharing relatable anecdotes, listening with empathy, and bringing them around to her point of view. And while she did attend Princeton and Harvard Law, it was through determination and hard work, not connections or privilege. And she was and has always been unapologetically proud of her academic and professional achievements. But rather than crow about them, she uses herself as an example to encourage others to dream big. Because if a girl from the South Side could do it, other promising young people can as well. "If my future were determined just by my performance on a standardized test, I wouldn't be here. I guarantee you that."

**What's Your M.O.?** It's hard to suffer fools. Michelle certainly has had to deal with her share of them, from online trolls to various politicians. When you meet someone who triggers your internal eye roll, keep in mind two things: compassion and persuasion. Listen to what someone is trying to convey to you, see them as a human being with opinions and thoughts that are entirely valid—even if they've gotten the facts mixed up or flat-out wrong. Ask questions, stay present. This is the compassion component. View the interaction as a teachable moment, an opportunity to present your case, appealing to what's important to them while supporting your view with actual facts and reason. See the end goal as sharing new information and opening someone's eyes or expanding their worldview, rather than smothering them with your massive intellect. Even when it comes to correcting someone's pronunciation or misuse of a

*"What I learned growing up is that if I'm not going to get my butt kicked every day after school, I can't flaunt my intelligence in front of peers who are struggling with a whole range of things. So you've got to be smart without acting smart. [It's like] speaking two languages."*

word, think about whether it matters in the big picture and whether the person would want to know the correct use of the word or phrase. Sometimes, they just might not care, as hard as it is for you to accept. Never dull your shine, but use it strategically. No one likes a know-it-all, but everyone can appreciate someone sincerely interested in having a dialogue, rather than delivering a lecture.

*"Education is the single most important civil rights issue that we face today."*

*"I started thinking about the fact that I went to some of the best schools in the country and I have no idea what I want to do. That kind of stuff got me worked up because I thought, 'This isn't education. You can make money and have a nice degree. But what are you learning about giving back to the world, and finding your passion and letting that guide you, as opposed to the school you got into?'"*

# You want to learn something new but don't know where to look.

"I used to hate the question, 'What do you want to be when you grow up?' because it assumes that at some point you stop becoming and you just *are* something. And that would be a sad thing to think that 'this is it.'" Like many smart women, Michelle Obama knows that our evolution continues throughout our life and that evolution is a result of experience, taking chances, and continued education. When she decided to create a White House kitchen garden, she needed help. Remember, she's a city girl. She consulted gardeners, chefs, and beekeepers, studied the history of White House gardens, and boned up on soil and hardiness zones. On the campaign trail, she studied policy papers and honed her own opinion after reviewing source material and talking with subject experts. Her post-White House life also reflects her commitment to learning and evolving: she announced the Barack Obama Presidential Library with Barack, regularly delivers speeches on topics dear to her heart, and continues to work to improve the health and education of women and children.

*What's Your M.O.?* Learning is exciting; personal development is deeply satisfying. And learning new skills or knowledge doesn't have to happen in a college classroom. Make a list of all the things you'd like to learn, no matter how silly. Have you always wanted to knit or paint or garden or play the guitar or bake the perfect pastry? Do you wish you knew more about science and astronomy or wine and its appellations? Want to learn conversational Spanish to help you in your travels? Now, look at that list and tap your community. Reach out to any people in your life who might be able to teach you or at least refer you to someone or someplace who can. Check your local college and community center for non-credit courses or lecture series. Attend book readings. Scan the calendar of local libraries and museums for talks or events. And there's always the internet: do an online search for classes in your area. You'll be surprised at how many opportunities to learn are lurking in your own backyard. Remember, you're still becoming!

*"Maybe you feel like your destiny was written the day you were born and you ought to just rein in your hopes and scale back your dreams. But if any of you are thinking that way, I'm here to tell you:* **Stop it."**

## You get easily distracted when studying, writing, or reviewing any document of length.

Michelle's time has always been precious, so she's learned to make the most of every moment. That said, she's human and there are days when

she's not operating at her usual 150 percent. So she needs a little motivation. As a kid, she was driven to get good grades, thinking there wasn't anything cooler than being a brainiac. As a lawyer and then executive, she found inspiration in her work and satisfaction in helping her community. As First Lady, seeing initiatives like Let's Move and the White House kitchen garden bloom and take root

kept her engaged and committed. By visualizing the results of her efforts, she was able to stay focused.

**What's Your M.O.?** Like Michelle, your productivity can soar if you keep your eye on the prize. If it's not obvious, create a carrot for yourself. When you complete a huge project, reward yourself with a day off or a meal at your favorite restaurant. When you write 500 words for that report or book project, take a walk for 15 minutes or watch baby goat videos online. Even so, staying focused is challenging, so break your work up into small, doable pieces. Set a timer and work in 15-minute increments. Make a list of your biggest distractions and then see how you can mitigate them.

> *"I never cut class . . . I loved getting As. I liked being smart. I loved being on time. I loved getting my work done. I thought being smart was cooler than anything in the world."*

If your office is noisy, invest in sound-canceling headphones. Turn off your devices and allocate certain times of day to checking and returning e-mails. If you must, download an app that will shut off all your social media or internet connection for a specified time. Experiment with different techniques for keeping your butt in your chair and always keep visualizing the satisfaction or success that comes with completing the task at hand.

## You have a hard time speaking up and being heard. Sometimes you feel that you're invisible.

Michelle has never been a shy retiring wallflower. She may not be an extreme extrovert but she has always felt comfortable taking a seat at the table and speaking her mind. Her parents made sure of that. Her mother, Marian, recalled resenting that she herself couldn't say what she felt when she was a child. She raised Craig and Michelle to speak up and question things. Michelle learned this lesson well. Today, she's strategic and careful with her words. She knows the value of listening to others and thinking about the key points she wants to get across. When she speaks, her words have that much more impact. She knows her value and intelligence and that guides her speech.

*What's Your M.O.?* Have you heard of the law of attraction? Basically, it means that whatever you put out into the world will result in the same coming back to you. So if you're focusing on the positive, positive things will result. If you feel invisible, that's how you might be perceived by others. The problem is that this builds on itself, right? If you feel overlooked or slighted, you get that much more down on yourself, which then just perpetuates the problem. Know your value. Say it like a mantra. Ask to be included in meetings. Write down your key talking points for reference. Start small, speaking up amongst friends and family. If you're in a relationship with an extrovert who steamrolls you, pick your moment, begin by saying her name, and tell her you want to make a point. Saying someone's name grabs her attention and makes her pause, giving you an opening in the conversation. Next, work on communicating more with your manager and colleagues in one-on-one situations. Knowing your value, your opinion, and key facts, jump into the conversation during work meetings, conferences, and volunteer committees. You will improve with practice and slowly feel more comfortable driving the conversation. You have value. You are seen.

*"I admit it: I am louder than the average human being and have no fear of speaking my mind. These traits don't come from the color of my skin but from an unwavering belief in my own intelligence."*

# You have always been interested in mentoring but don't know if you have any advice of value.

Michelle Obama is all about mentoring. She did it while working high-level jobs in Chicago, she promoted it during her time as executive director of Public Allies (a mentoring and internship program), and continued to mentor youth during her time as First Lady. Krsna Golden was in the first class of Public Allies. He wasn't an obvious choice—he had some sketchy activities in his background—but Michelle saw his potential even if he didn't always. Her belief in him, along with her straight talk, helped him to win an award that took him to Washington and then participate in a cultural exchange program in Germany. She has always made time for mentoring, even while raising two daughters, because she knows how important it is for our youth to have people to not only look up to, but to talk to. "Even though our children are connecting in ways we never imagined," she said, "you've got an entire generation of young people truly in desperate need of a friend. Someone they can trust, an example they can follow." That someone can be you.

> *"If there's anybody telling you that you're not college material—anyone— I want you to brush 'em off. Prove them wrong."*

***What's Your M.O.?*** You may not have a powerful job or consider yourself an expert in a field or industry. But like most women, you don't know how much you *do* know, based on life experience as well as your career. Kids or young adults at the onset of their careers need advice, yes, but they also need support, encouragement, and a constant champion. Sometimes they just need a sounding board. Think about it: What do *you* wish you had known when you started out? To take more risks? To trust your instincts? What do you see in young people today that you'd like to adjust? What would you like to learn from them? Wouldn't it be wonderful to simply be another person in their life whom they can trust, respect, and count on? Mentoring is a two-way street and you'll find it to be a gift you both give and receive.

*"Right now, there are 62 million girls worldwide that aren't in school for a variety of different reasons. So much could be corrected in the world if girls were educated and had power over their lives. My message to kids here is don't take your education for granted. Because there are girls around the world who would die to get the education we have."*

# Health + Wellness

*Michelle Obama* cultivated a culture of fitness

and health during her time as First Lady.

She practiced what she preached, spearheading

a public health campaign designed to reduce

childhood obesity and planting an organic kitchen

garden on the White House grounds.

*"I have never felt more confident in myself, more clear on who I am as a woman. But I am constantly thinking about my own health and making sure that I'm eating right and getting exercise and watching the aches and pains. I want to be this really fly 80-, 90-year-old."*

## You don't have any spare time to exercise.

When Michelle was in high school, it was so noisy in her small household that she set her alarm earlier so she could study in peace. When she found her schedule increasingly full as a working mom, she did the same for exercise, fitting in trips to the gym around her appointments and responsibilities. She carved out extra time in the day for herself, hitting the

gym at 4:30 a.m. to meet with a trainer while Barack handled morning feedings. Exercising as her first activity had the added benefit of setting a great tone for the day, as she headed off to work high on endorphins and a sense of satisfaction and well-being.

***What's Your M.O.?*** If you weren't sure that Michelle Obama was a superheroine by now, finding out that she gets up before dawn to work out probably seals the deal. If you are unwilling to trade sleep for kettlebells, you're not alone. That said, if you can even get up 15 minutes early, you can stretch or meditate to start your day. If your commute is short enough, trade your car for a bike or tennis shoes. If you're stuck at a desk, make sure to get up every hour to walk and stretch and take the stairs over the elevator whenever possible. All this movement matters. And if there is a yoga or Pilates studio nearby, consider dropping in for lunch-time classes or sessions right after work. You'll be forced to leave the office at a reasonable hour and you can take the class on the way home. Once in the house, it's far too easy to blow off exercise, particularly if a new Netflix series is waiting to be binge watched.

> *"Women in particular need to keep an eye on their physical and mental health, because if we're scurrying to and from appointments and errands, we don't have a lot of time to take care of ourselves. We need to do a better job of putting ourselves higher on our own 'to-do' list."*

# HOW TO GET MICHELLE OBAMA ARMS

///////////////////////////////

*You can watch Michelle kicking butt (actually, kicking a punching bag) in a workout video on YouTube while her trainer talks you through her workout. To get toned arms, try these two exercises:*

**Hammer curl:** Using a pair of dumbbells (using five- to eight-pound weights), hold one in each hand with your arms hanging straight at your sides.

With palms facing in, slowly raise the weight in your left hand as high as you can in front of you, bending your elbow and bringing the dumbbell toward your shoulder while keeping your upper arm still.

As you lower the dumbbell and return your left arm to its starting position, curl the weight in your right hand. Alternate arms for one minute. **Try for five sets.**

**Chest fly:** Lying on a bench or the floor, bend your knees. Grab a dumbbell with each hand and raise your arms above you until they are parallel. Slowly lower both arms until they are level with your body and at a 90-degree angle to your body. Raise your arms to the original position. **Repeat for one minute or 20 reps. Do five sets.**

**Just do it.** There are so many great exercises you can do at home or at the gym to tone your arms. Just grab your dumbbells and check out the exercises that work your arms, chest, and shoulders. You'll be going sleeveless in no time!

## You hate to exercise and the gym is so expensive anyway.

Unlike many of us, Michelle finds working out therapeutic and for many years, fit in an early-morning workout with her trainer, doing strength and cardio at the gym. As part of her Let's Move campaign, however, Michelle worked hard to show America that there are all sorts of avenues for activity and fitness, be it hula hooping, dancing, playing basketball, yoga, swimming, or cycling. The trick is to find what jazzes you, what doesn't feel like work, and has an element of fun to it. Chances are that you'll stick with it and become even more motivated once you see the health benefits of exercise.

*"We can't lie around on the couch eating French fries and candy bars, and expect our kids to eat carrots and run around the block. But too often, that's exactly what we're doing."*

### What's Your M.O.?

Let's break this down. First, you hate to exercise. If you lack motivation, it may be that it seems overwhelming to work out, or you're fried from work and other responsibilities. Start small! Try walking or a slow jog for five minutes initially, and slowly build up time or distance or incline. The same goes for any activity: turn on the radio and dance to your favorite song, and, over time, to your favorite album. Put it on your daily schedule in a time slot that's doable and give yourself that time to care for your body. Okay, next: you think the gym is pricey. Not always. There are plenty of gyms that charge $20 a month and even that is often negotiable. Sign up for a trial membership or just three months and take advantage of the trainer there if the first session is free. She can create a chart for cardio and circuit training so you can do it yourself on subsequent visits. When it comes to health clubs, the trick is to not commit to a long-term contract because we've all paid for a membership we didn't use. That's most definitely a waste of money. If you really don't want to shell out any money for a gym, create a workout you can do at home or outside. Jump on a bike or hit the trail for free. Find a used treadmill or stationary bike if you want to work out at home. Check out some online mat Pilates or yoga you can do in your living room. Finally, rope in a friend to be a workout buddy: you can motivate and support each other in your fitness goals while spending time together each day. It really is hard to stay motivated when it comes to working out, but if you can find inexpensive activities that you love and take it slow, you have a shot of making it an essential and welcome part of your daily routine.

*"I have freed myself to put me on the priority list and say, yes, I can make choices that make me happy, and it will ripple and benefit my kids, my husband, and my physical health. That's hard for women to own; we're not taught to do that."*

## You try to eat well but all bets are off when you go out to dinner.

When Michelle was juggling a high-powered job and parenting (Barack was often away when the state and then U.S. Senate was in session), she found herself picking up fast food through the drive-thru or loading up her shopping cart with microwavable meals that were quick and easy. After her pediatrician told her that her daughters had high BMIs (body mass indices), she made it a priority to eat healthy meals at home with the family and save dessert and snacks for an occasional treat. And healthy, nutritious meals can also be a snap—Michelle often relies on a favorite chili recipe (see page 103) for a dinner that is always a crowd pleaser. Learning how to eat healthy at home gives the whole family tools to navigate a menu when dining out.

**What's Your M.O.?** Eating out seems like an indulgent treat, but if it becomes frequent, it pays

> *"When we engage children in harvesting our gardens—when we teach them about where their food comes from, how to prepare it, and how to grow it themselves—they reap the benefits well into the future. These early lessons about nutrition can affect the choices they make about what they eat for the rest of their lives—and that can determine what they feed their own children decades from now."*

to know your way around a menu. Here's where knowledge is power. Learn the difference between grilled, sautéed, and pan-fried, for example, and ask for sauces and dressings on the side. You'd be surprised to find out how much butter or oil might be lurking in that plate of steak frites. Choose where you want to indulge. If dessert's your thing, opt for grilled veggies and a simply prepared protein. If you are all about savory, skip the sweets and order the chicken potpie but add a side salad. Try to get something raw and unadorned on your plate each time. And if you are picking the restaurant, choose carefully. Opt for a place that specializes in farm-to-table seasonal cooking, for example, over an Italian restaurant known for its bottomless pasta. If you do dive into a breadbasket or plate of fettuccine, your body will often let you know if it was a bad idea. Aside from the calories or cholesterol, certain foods can trigger mild allergic reactions, bloating, and gas. And while you can live with the discomfort, you may decide that "eating clean" is preferable to the distress, logy feeling, and extra weight brought on by regular rendezvouses with your favorite wood-fired pizza.

*"We would never dream of letting our kids skip going to the doctor or learning how to add and subtract just because they don't like it. And the same thing is true about eating healthy. We know we have to be firm."*

# OBAMA TURKEY CHILI

/////////////////////////////

*Michelle loves to make this healthy and easy meal in the Obama household.*

*Serves 4–6*

## You'll need:

1 large onion, chopped

1 green pepper, chopped

Several cloves of garlic, chopped

1 tablespoon olive oil

1 pound ground turkey

¼ teaspoon ground cumin

¼ teaspoon ground oregano

¼ teaspoon ground turmeric

¼ teaspoon ground basil

1 tablespoon chili powder

3 tablespoons red-wine vinegar

5–6 tomatoes, chopped

1 can red kidney beans

1. In a large skillet, sauté the onion, green pepper, and garlic in olive oil until soft.

2. Add the ground turkey and brown.

3. Combine the spices and add to skillet.

4. Add the red-wine vinegar.

5. Add the tomatoes and let simmer until cooked down.

6. Add the kidney beans; simmer a few more minutes.

7. Serve over white or brown rice. Garnish with grated cheddar cheese, onions, and sour cream.

# WHAT WOULD MICHELLE OBAMA PLANT?
## *A peek at the White House Kitchen Garden*
//////////////////////////////

In Michelle's book, ***American Grown: The Story of the White House Kitchen Garden and Gardens Across America***, the First Lady takes us behind the scenes. She discusses her desire to create a garden for her family but one that would also provide inspiration to the nation, instruction to kids, and produce to local food banks. She invited local kids to join her in the planting, weeding, and harvest, so they could all experience the pleasure of watching crops grow and eating the literal fruits of their labors. She often took Bo and then Sunny with her to the vegetable beds. As the dogs wandered the garden paths, Michelle pulled weeds or picked ripe vegetables and fruit. What exactly did Michelle plant? Gardening is a year-round activity at the White House, so seasonal produce is planted in the beds, with certain crops rotated throughout the year for maximum growth.

**Spring:** Lettuces and greens of all kinds, broccoli, cauliflower, beets, peas, herbs, rhubarb

**Summer:** Tomatoes, eggplant, squash, corn, beans, sweet potatoes, onions, peppers, cucumbers, herbs, strawberries, raspberries, blueberries

**Autumn:** Tomatoes, eggplant, corn, beans, pumpkin, lettuces, sweet potatoes, kale, Swiss chard, bok choy, Brussels sprouts, peppers, herbs, strawberries, raspberries, blueberries

**Winter:** Winter rye, red clover, greens and lettuces (including endive, spinach, radicchio, kale, Swiss chard, collards), garlic, lavender, berries

## Stress is wreaking havoc on your body in new and sneaky ways, be it tight muscles, a short fuse, binge eating, smoking, acid reflux.

Michelle possesses a remarkable ability to always looks unflappable. But she's human and, like you, she worries. She worried about Barack's security when he was elected president. She worries about her kids. She has had a stressful schedule for most of her adult life. But through it all, she has managed to control her stress through exercise and the support of family and friends. She has never acted the martyr, suffering silently. Rather, she speaks up, reaches out, and takes care to take care of herself first before tending to her loved ones. She knows that you are no good to anyone if you're not tending to your own well-being.

*What's Your M.O.?* Stress is no bueno. It has a deleterious effect on our mental, physical, and spiritual states. And when we get stressed, we often act out with even more unhealthy behavior to temporarily assuage our anxiety. Driving home from a 12-hour day, it's easy to order a pizza and then plow through the entire pie. Or light up a cigarette after being stuck in traffic for two hours. It's time to flip the switch on what we consider indulgences. Instead of picking up a pizza, make one of your favorite recipes and eat at home. Rather than light up to calm down, inform the household that you are unavailable for the next hour and take a bubble bath. For longer-term solutions to stress, embrace exercise and alternative therapies. Breathing, meditation, tai chi, and yoga can counter the effects of stress and even give you strategies for minimizing and stopping stress in its tracks. Taking care of yourself is what's truly indulgent and pampering.

## You're stuck in a rut, making the same bad choices and mulling problems over and over in your head without any answers.

As a young mother, Michelle was frequently left to parent solo as Barack campaigned and commuted to Springfield and then Washington, D.C. She couldn't figure out how to juggle everything and was perpetually frustrated by her husband's absence. She kept cycling through various options, never coming up with a solution that would fix everything. She could become a stay-at-home mom, but she loved to work. And it seemed almost impossible to be a great, nurturing mother and have a full-time career. She wanted Barack to change—become tidier, be home more—but didn't want him to sacrifice his ambitions either. Eventually, she realized that she had to shift her perspective and adjust her expectations. She learned to let things go, changed up her schedule to give herself some down time, and looked for support elsewhere. She could be crazy, angry, and righteous, or she could get help and make peace.

*What's Your M.O.?* You feel stuck in a loop. You seem to keep dating the same toxic person. You wake up in the middle of the night and worry an issue from every angle until the sun comes up. Your friends have been patient but even they are getting tired of hearing you obsess over the same thing. Stage your own intervention, gathering your tribe to help remind you of your amazing qualities and to problem solve together. Acknowledge that you're having a hard time and ask them to help you break the loop and get on with your life. Give them a script to use when you are in crisis so when you call, they can help steer you away from unhealthy thinking or behavior. Consider therapy or coaching as well to help you figure out the root of your problem and how to move your life forward. There's no shame in seeking professional help for the short term or on an ongoing basis to support you in becoming your best self. Life is too short to be in a painful holding pattern.

> *"Music is my best de-stresser in life. The times when Barack and I are at our most relaxed are when we invite some friends over who we have known forever. And you put a little music on top of that? Some good food? It renews your spirit to get back in the game."*

# Sense *of a* Woman

Being a woman is hard. Duh, right?

*Michelle Obama* is a global champion

of girls and women, continually

encouraging them to reach beyond

what's expected toward what's possible.

**You wore a pussy hat and marched. You want to continue to support women's rights, but your motivation is flagging.**

The fight is long and ongoing. Michelle knows this from experience. Springboarding from her South Side roots, she attended Princeton and Harvard Law School and was faced with an extensive course load. Despite that, she carved out time to get involved with campus organizations and community service. The community and meaningful work actually buoyed and supported her academic career. She focused her thesis on identity and purpose among black Princeton graduates. She found a way to merge her values and passions with her work.

> *"You need more women who are going to push if they have the leverage. Not everyone has the leverage, so you have to push for the women who don't."*

# "As women, we must stand up for each other."

**What's Your M.O.?** Michael Moore made a wonderful metaphor comparing activism to an orchestra. It's okay to take a breath, because others are still making music. Add your voice back in when you can. On that note, use your online and IRL community to stay motivated. Pick one main cause and devote your energies to it because, heaven knows, thinking about all the problems in the country and the world is enough to put anyone into the fetal position. If women's rights are dear to your heart, volunteer and donate to organizations like Planned Parenthood. If you are focused on racial discrimination, look online to see how you can support the ACLU, Southern Poverty Law Center, or Black Lives Matter movement. These organizations can help you get started, match you with like-minded individuals, and support you in your activism.

**It sounds silly, but you honestly don't know how to take time for yourself and practice self-care.**

It's hard for a working mom to find time for herself. Michelle's no different. But she knows the importance of taking care of yourself first, because you're not going to be your best self with your friends, family, and job if you're frazzled or worn out. It's not selfish, it's practical. With a packed schedule, Michelle always creates time to work out because for her, "exercise is more than just physical—it's therapeutic." She finds other ways to enjoy meaningful "me" time as well. Getting together with her trusted girlfriends—"pulling in people in my life who give me strength and joy"—recharges her. Not only that, it allows her an opportunity to talk with other women about work, family, relationships, and other important topics. Michelle is a people person, which is why mentoring is another way she feeds her spirit. Add to that listening to her favorite music and gardening, and Michelle has found small but impactful ways to take care of herself on the daily. And she doesn't discount the restorative properties of a guilty pleasure, like binge-watching *Scandal* during a long flight when she has some unexpected down time.

> *"My happiness isn't connected to my husband's or my boss's or my children's behavior. You have control over your own actions, your own well-being."*

> *"People told me, 'You can do it all.*
> *Just stay the course, get your education and you can*
> *raise a child, stay thin, be in shape, love your man,*
> *look good, and raise healthy children.' That was a lie."*

**What's Your M.O.?** Figure out what recharges your batteries and centers you. Once you've determined what revives and nourishes you, you can then figure out how to make small changes in your schedule that will support you. Sometimes, you just need a few minutes. Set a timer to remind you every hour to focus on your breath for one minute. Download some apps that can help you meditate, drift off to sleep, or coach you to a 5k. If you commute, use the drive to listen to your favorite podcasts or sing show tunes at the top of your lungs. Find five trusty recipes that only take 15 minutes to prepare. Take a walk before work or after dinner. Turn off your devices and take a bedtime bath. If you commit to slipping in self-care on a daily basis, they will become rituals you look forward to, in body and spirit. Remember, it's not selfish, it's practical to make yourself a priority!

## You don't know how to be a sexual person without feeling judged.

One need only look at Michelle and Barack Obama to see that they have a pretty juicy relationship. She calls him "swagalicious," swooning over his walk. "Good lord. Watching my husband walk off of Marine One and go to the Oval Office, it's like, mmm, mmm, mmm." She is careful not to get too racy in public, but she also doesn't hide her sexuality or womanliness, wearing form-fitting clothing and engaging in public discourse about the need to treat women's bodies, ambitions, and intellect with respect.

*What's Your M.O.?* You've come a long way, baby. But we still have a long way to go. Slut-shaming is a real thing, and it's unfortunate. Like many issues, when it comes to sex, there's a double standard. Men are swinging singles; women are sluts. Sometimes, we even judge ourselves, thinking we shouldn't dress or flirt a certain way, shouldn't be sexual. But we are sexual beings, as much as we are intelligent or emotional beings. It's part of our nature, and to deny that part of ourselves means we are dulling our shine, hiding our truth. Do your best to tune out the negative messages and focus on your inner voice. How do you want to live your life? Authentically and abundantly? Do you want to own your body and your choices? While you may suffer some blowback when you wear a revealing outfit or make the first move or play the field, the only voice you should listen to is your own.

"Part of what
we fought for is
choice, not
just one definition
of what it means
to be a woman."

## Yet again, a guy is mansplaining at you.

Most likely, Michelle has faced a mansplainer or two throughout her academic and professional career. Even as a child, people were more interested in what her older brother had to say. "I got the message that I shouldn't take up too much space in this world. That I should speak softly and rarely." We know how well that worked out! In fact, we women have all been condescended to by men at one time or another, told to be quiet, told our voice isn't important. President Obama's female staffers experienced exclusion and mansplaining, so they came up with a strategy. Every time a woman made a key point in a meeting, another woman would pick up the baton, repeating the point and crediting the author. They called this "amplification," and it served the dual purpose of acknowledging the female contribution to the room while preventing a man from taking credit for it. Clever!

*What's Your M.O.?* Aargh! We have been complacent "good girls" long enough. Research shows that in meetings, women talk 25 percent to men's 75 percent. Chances are good that a male colleague or friend will talk over you or mansplain because they, just like us, have been conditioned to do so. It doesn't make him a jerk, necessarily, and it's up to you to break him of this obnoxious habit. If he wants to tell you what it's like for women these days, counter with personal anecdotes because your gender trumps him on this point. If he questions sexism or feminism, hit him with statistics. Yep, the female salary is holding steady at 89 cents on the dollar. It's particularly galling when they mansplain about your area of expertise. The best thing to do to shut them down is to ask a super-specific question that only an expert like you would know to ask or answer. Even if he can cobble together a response, he'll look at you in a new way. If nothing works, ignore them. When they mansplain, we go high.

*"The work always continues. We're never done. We can never be complacent and think we've arrived as women...Because we have seen in recent times how quickly things can be taken away if we aren't vigilant, if we don't know our history, if we don't continue the work."*

# You really need to find a supportive circle of women.

"There is nothing in this world more valuable than friendships. Without them you have nothing." Michelle Obama wrote that on her senior yearbook page at Princeton. And she's continued to cherish her female friendships, many of whom she's known since her college or Chicago days. As First Lady, she often turned to them for support and to stay grounded. They were frequent visitors in the White House, and their laughter ricocheted throughout the halls. Her closest friends are also highly accomplished women, some of whom Michelle tapped to work with her in the White House, ensuring a staff of loyal, trusted, and highly qualified women. We all can't hire our closest friends, but we can look to bring more and more aspirational women into our lives.

> "My ability to get through my day greatly depends upon the relationships that I have with women: my mother, my aunt, my girlfriends, my neighbors, the mothers in my children's school... In these women I find a place of comfort and sanity and peace like no other."

*What's Your M.O.?* Women are natural connectors and nurturers and there's nothing better than finding your tribe. Sometimes that's hard, however. Maybe you moved to a new town and your East Coast energy doesn't jive with your new city's attitude. Maybe you keep trying to put a group together and it fizzles every time. Or maybe you've been knee-deep in parenting or a stressful job that has left little time for new relationships. Whatever the case, you need to amp up the estrogen and find or create a community of women. Think beyond the book club (although those can be awesome). What are your interests? If you're crafty, join the weekly knitting circle at your local yarn shop. Politics? Look for a local chapter of NOW or the League of Women Voters or volunteer at Planned Parenthood. If you're active, there are running, cycling, hiking, mountain climbing, and skiing groups in many towns. Craving something more spiritually gratifying? Start regularly attending a place of worship, a drum circle, a prayer group, or a meditation group. These groups will put you on the path of assembling a circle of friends

who are smart, interesting, and share similar interests and outlooks. And think beyond your town: Rekindle friendships with classmates or women from cities you used to live in or jobs you used to have. It's powerful to have people in your life who have known you for decades—they are like family. Track down a few long-lost pals through social media or mutual friends, and rekindle your friendship through regular e-mails, video chats, or actual handwritten letters.

*"My message to women: Do what makes you feel good, because there'll always be someone who thinks you should do it differently. Whether your choices are hits or misses, at least they're your own."*

"We as a nation benefit from every girl whose potential is fulfilled; from every woman whose talent is tapped. We benefit as a nation. We as a nation benefit from their intelligence, from their hard work, from their creativity, from their leadership."

# A Call *to* Action

With her own life as an example, *Michelle*

has continued to urge Americans to get involved,

strive, be the change they want to see in

the world, and when things get tough, to dust

themselves off and start again.

# "When they go low, we go high."

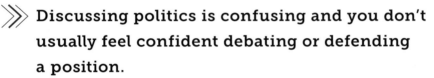 **Discussing politics is confusing and you don't usually feel confident debating or defending a position.**

Michelle Obama is nothing if not a diligent student. As she did throughout her academic career, she prepares and studies and researches and interviews people. Even when she delivers a speech, she rehearses and refines it until her words perfectly convey her message. She is not so arrogant as to think she already has all the answers. Nope. Throughout her life, she has pinpointed her weaknesses and the holes in her knowledge base. Armed with that information, she'd set about filling in the gaps. As a black woman growing up on the South Side of Chicago, she *had* to be more committed, more tenacious, more determined, more prepared. So she was ready when it came time to give a speech, be interviewed, or debate political issues. And if she didn't know something, she asked more questions.

**What's Your M.O.?** Talking politics is tricky and millions of people shy away from political conversations, thinking things will become heated or they won't be able to articulate their position. There's always that special someone who will play devil's advocate, say provocative things, or refuse to back down from a position, no matter how flawed. Who wants to deal with that? But we are currently living in a politicized, polarized world, and you have passionate beliefs and positions. Do your research, which means coming out of your silo and reading credible news sources as well as reading or listening to journalists from across the aisle. (Keep your "enemies" closer, remember?) Then, start talking, at first with close friends in a space you know to be respectful and loving. Then start taking your show on the road, debating and trading positions with acquaintances and strangers, remembering to treat their views with consideration, no matter how heated the conversation gets. You know the drill: Go high even if they go low.

*"Do not ever let anyone ever make you feel*
*like you don't matter, or like you don't have a place*
*in our American story—because you do.*
*And you have a right to be exactly who you are.*
*But I also want to be very clear: This right*
*isn't just handed to you. No, this right has to be earned*
*every single day. You cannot take your*
*freedoms for granted."*

**You feel removed from much of the country but you'd like to find your "tribe" or cause and get involved.**

Michelle has frequently discussed the importance of reaching back, offering a helping hand to young people who are driven but perhaps have limited opportunity. And she walks her talk. When she was an undergrad at Princeton, Michelle spent time and worked at the Third World Center, building community and meeting students with a shared interest in social justice. During her time at Harvard Law School, Michelle volunteered at the Legal Aid Bureau, a student-run clinic for low-income clients. In her professional career and in her role as First Lady, she has continued to find ways to impact her community, often focusing on raising up ambitious kids in underserved communities.

***What's Your M.O.?*** Don't spend too much time looking for the perfect organization or opportunity, or you'll never get out of the gate. Instead, think about what issues are most important to you and then look for organizations that support your values and causes. Look in your own backyard, which can also be a digital space. There are loads of political interest groups on Facebook and other social networks. Jump into the conversation, look for opportunities that come up, ask if there's anyone in your geographical area who needs help. Inquire if your company does any ongoing initiatives or service projects, and if not, perhaps you can start one with its support. Start local and you'll soon find that your efforts are worthwhile and meaningful to you and your community.

*"I did exactly what leaders in my community told me to do. They said to do your best in school, work hard, study, get into the best schools you can get into, and when you do that, baby, you bring that education back and you work in your communities."*

# You are considering running for office but don't know where to start.

Michelle has said she has no plans to run for public office because she doesn't want to subject her family to that sort of scrutiny again. But she was Barack's biggest champion during his senate and presidential campaigns. The Obamas assembled a team of trusted advisers and took to the campaign trail with a message of "Yes, we can." And yes, she did. Michelle was often Barack's most effective asset, delivering speeches to crowds large and small. She wasn't a born politician, but she leveraged her strengths and interests. With verbal skills and quick thinking honed from her years as an attorney and an interest in social justice for all Americans, Michelle was able to speak powerfully from her heart and draw from her own experiences. Her message resonated with voters and her authenticity shone through.

*What's Your M.O.?* If you're considering running for office, clearly you're fired up. Let's do this thing! Like Michelle, be a tenacious student and do your research. Interview a local elected official and ask frank questions about time commitment, campaign strategies and expenses, things that surprised her, privacy, the challenges and rewards, other considerations. The Internet offers some great resources for aspiring candidates. For example, Emily's List offers training for women ready to run for office. Your state offers information online about how to go about becoming a candidate. Money is a consideration; find out from the secretary of state or county clerk how much the previous candidates spent on their campaigns. That will give you some idea of your fundraising goals. Now, think about all the issues that are important to you. Start jotting those down and you'll eventually have a comprehensive platform. Start building a base of supporters, starting with friends, families, colleagues, acquaintances, fellow congregants, neighbors, parents, and expand from there. Listen to their issues and take them to heart. At this point, you should be ready to mount a viable campaign that represents your core values and the issues important to your constituents.

*"True leadership often happens with the smallest acts, in the most unexpected places, by the most unlikely individuals."*

**A close friend or family member has political views that are completely opposite from yours. Every time you talk, you feel more and more alienated.**

Michelle has said she's louder than most, that she has no fear of speaking up and speaking out. This comes out of a childhood spent talking and debating issues around the dinner table. She was taken seriously and encouraged to voice her opinion. This served her well when she entered the

White House and had to advocate for initiatives that Republicans opposed. When she was campaigning for Hillary Clinton, she spoke out against sexual harassment and disparaging talk against women after Donald Trump's *Access Hollywood* video surfaced. Out of office, she still speaks her mind and stumps for causes she's passionate about. Through it all, she never makes it personal, attacking or belittling someone for beliefs or

opinions diametrically opposed to her positions. She stays on message, keeping it classy without backing off or backing down. While we don't have a view into how she deals with close friends or family who are on the opposite end of the political spectrum, the world noticed that she gets on like a house on fire with former President George W. Bush, a man with many political beliefs at odds with her own. But she focused on the things that unite them— love of country, a sense of humor—and was able to forge a friendship based on mutual respect.

***What's Your M.O.?*** In this political climate, it's likely that you have discovered that some of your friends and family have *very* different political views than you do. Perhaps it wasn't a big deal in the past, or you weren't aware of their politics. Now that you are, you want to either scream at them or ghost them. Here's the thing: you can unfriend and unfollow all you want but these are loved ones, people you know have good hearts. Hold onto that. That said, don't shy away from difficult conversations. Start from a place of respect and stay calm. They have good hearts. Challenge their beliefs but do it with respect, sticking to the facts as best you can. Don't embarrass or shame them. You can't change their thinking or persuade them if you put them on the defensive. Rather, work to understand why they think they way they do. Ask them some open-ended questions, such as "Have you always felt that way? If not, what changed for you?" "Tell me why you support that candidate." "What issue in this election is most important to you?" Respect their background and personal experiences. They have good hearts. If they start citing "facts" you know are untrue, invite them to share their sources and you'll do the same. If you can provide them with five credible outlets to every wingnut source they supply, you might, just might, get them to look beyond their silo of news outlets. Remember, they have good hearts.

*"You may not always have a comfortable life and you will not always be able to solve all of the world's problems at once but don't ever underestimate the importance you can have because history has shown us that courage can be contagious and hope can take on a life of its own."*

**You don't feel that your voice or vote makes any difference.**

Michelle and Barack Obama have lived their lives by the belief that one voice can effect change, be it on a small or sweeping scale. Michelle's involvement in mentoring programs, for example, had a profound impact on the youth she mentored both on the South Side of Chicago and in the White House. Barack's experience with community organizing created a movement that resulted in the historic election of the first black president. So don't let Michelle hear you say that your contribution doesn't matter.

*"Any woman who voted against Hillary Clinton voted against their own voice."*

**What's Your M.O.?** It's easy to get discouraged when you see legislators making decisions that benefit powerful interest groups and the wealthy instead of their constituents. But you need only look around you in your community or in the news to see stories of ordinary people moving the needle. The 2017 Women's March, vocal town halls, and increased activism led to politicians stepping away from party loyalty and instead advocating for their districts and states. When you speak out to one or many, know that your message can resonate with them long after. Words have the power to move people, literally and figuratively. When you get discouraged, think about your favorite lines from poems, books, and famous speeches: "I have a dream," "Yes, we can," "When they go low, we go high." When you vote, know that each and every vote goes toward creating a mandate that reflects your values. Many an election has been determined by the fewest of votes. Exercise the privilege we as Americans have to make our voices and vote count. As Barack said, "Don't boo. Vote."

> "I want our young people to know that they matter. That they belong. So don't be afraid. Do you hear me? Young people, don't be afraid. Be focused. Be determined. Be hopeful. Be empowered. Empower yourselves with a good education. Then get out there and use that education to build a country worthy of your boundless promise. Lead by example with hope, never fear, and know that I will be with you, rooting for you and working to support you for the rest of my life."

## You can't seem to motivate your friends or family to volunteer or donate to the cause.

Throughout her adult life, Michelle Obama has pushed initiatives that, on the surface, should have little opposition. Take healthy school lunches, for example. Who can argue with making meals healthier for school children? Well, she came up against opposition, legislators, lobby groups, and businesses that had their own opinions and agenda around those lunches.

*"When you've worked hard and done well and walked through that doorway of opportunity, you do not slam it shut behind you. No. You reach back, and you give other folks the same chances that helped you succeed."*

She did what any passionate advocate would do: she stumped relentlessly, working to build public support for her Let's Move initiative. Now that her healthy lunch program has been rolled back, she continues to speak out in support of making students' lunches more nutritious.

***What's Your M.O.?*** You have your own passion projects and causes. Maybe it's fighting animal abuse or participating in Black Lives Matter or Indivisible events. Maybe it's just raising money for breast cancer research by running in the Race for the Cure. You start to wonder what's so hard about pledging a donation or joining the event. Judgment seeps in. In your mind, it's a cut and dried issue, and those who aren't with you are against you. Here's where you have to slow your roll. Passion is a wonderful thing, but you don't help your cause when you strong-arm or shame loved ones into participating. That said, don't throw in the towel; keep at it, but be respectful. Instead of asking a loved one to match your level of participation—a set up for failure all around—ask them to support *you*. Ask them for a modest donation, giving them a few statistics or facts about what their money is specifically going toward. Share your successes and challenges, particularly if you have had a difficult experience and need to vent. Ask them to join you for a meeting or a march, no strings attached. If they decline, accept—and respect—their decision. They aren't bad people, they just may have different priorities. Their redeeming quality is that they love you and will support you in your endeavors.

*"I might not live in the White House anymore,*
*but Barack and I are going to keep on celebrating you all*
*and supporting you and lifting you up no matter what*
*house we live in. Our belief in the power of education to*
*transform your lives is real and it's going to be at the*
*core of everything that we do going forward."*

## Conclusion

# *"Being your First Lady has been the greatest honor of my life, and I hope I've made you proud."*

So said Michelle in her last speech as First Lady. The honor has also been ours. She not only made us proud, she made us think, own our feminine power, and aspire to make a difference in the world, in ways both large and small. But in her words, we ain't done. She's still in the process of evolving. After leaving the White House, she's continued to speak out on issues close to her heart. And the wonderful thing for both her and us is that she has more freedom to speak her mind, work for change, and reach back to lift up more people. As she said at an AIA conference in 2017, "You don't have to be First Lady to influence." That's not only a prediction for her future, it's also a call to action for the women of America and the world.

***What's Your M.O.?*** Using the inimitable Michelle LaVaughn Robinson Obama as inspiration, how are you going to give back to the community, make our country reflect your values, and become your best self? How are you going to nurture your relationships and yourself? These are all lofty questions about long-term goals, but there is so much you can do starting right this minute. Using the examples and powerful statements provided by Michelle throughout this book, you have tools and advice for navigating challenging situations and living with abundance.

No matter where you're starting from in life, it's where you're *going* that matters. You're still becoming. You have the opportunity to redefine yourself every single day. Isn't that exciting? Whenever you need a little inspiration, dip back into this book so Michelle can help you back on course. And if things seem overwhelming, think about our First Lady and how she started from humble beginnings on Chicago's South Side. Armed with a steadfast belief in herself, she earned her spot at Princeton and Harvard Law, created a deeply satisfying and successful career while starting a family, and helped her husband to the highest office in the country. And that was just for starters! Michelle Obama has built an amazing life day by day, action by action, and so too can you. As she says, "Just try new things. Don't be afraid. Step out of your comfort zones and soar, all right?"

*"I will always be engaged in some way*
*in public service and public life. The minute I left my*
*corporate-law firm to work for the city, I never looked back.*
*I've always felt very alive using my gifts and talents*
*to help other people. I sleep better at night.*
*I'm happier."*

# Resources

## A SHORT READING LIST
*BOOKS ON WORK AND LEADERSHIP FOR WOMEN BY WOMEN*

*#GIRLBOSS*
by Sophia Amoruso

*All the Single Ladies:
Unmarried Women and the Rise
of an Independent Nation*
by Rebecca Traister

*Bossypants* by Tina Fey

*Coach Yourself to Success:
101 Tips from a Personal Coach
for Reaching Your Goals at
Work and in Life*
by Talane Miedaner

*Daring Greatly: How the Courage to
Be Vulnerable Transforms the Way We
Live, Love, Parent, and Lead*
by Brene Brown

*Double Bind: Women on Ambition*
edited by Robin Romm

*Feminist Fight Club:
An Office Survival Manual
(for a Sexist Workplace)*
by Jessica Bennett

*Grit: The Power of Passion
and Perseverance*
by Angela Duckworth

*Iron Butterflies: Women
Transforming Themselves
and the World*
by Birute Regine

*Lean In: Women, Work, and the
Will to Lead*
by Sheryl Sandberg

*Nice Girls Don't Get the Corner Office*
by Lois P. Frankel

*Radical Candor: Be a Kickass Boss
without Losing Your Humanity*
by Kim Scott

*Thrive: The Third Metric to
Redefining Success and Creating
a Life of Well-Being, Wisdom,
and Wonder*
by Arianna Huffington

*Why Not Me?*
by Mindy Kaling

*You Are a Badass: How to Stop
Doubting Your Greatness and Start
Living an Awesome Life*
by Jen Sincero

# AN INCOMPLETE READING LIST
## FOR EVERY AMERICAN

*Alexander Hamilton*
by Ron Chernow

*All the King's Men*
by Robert Penn Warren

*All the President's Men*
by Bob Woodward and Carl Bernstein

*The American Spirit: Who We Are
and What We Stand For* and any
presidential biography
by David McCullough

*Angels in America*
by Tony Kushner

*The Bill of Rights*

*The Constitution*

*Between the World and Me* and
*We Were Eight Years in Power:
An American Tragedy*
by Ta-Nehisi Coates

*The Death and Life of Great
American Cities*
by Jane Jacobs

*The Declaration of Independence*

*Diplomacy* by Henry Kissinger

*The Emancipation Proclamation*

*The Fire Next Time*
by James Baldwin

*Freedom for the Thought That We Hate:
A Biography of the First Amendment*
by Anthony Lewis

*The Greatest Generation*
by Tom Brokaw

*Hillbilly Elegy: A Memoir of a Family
and Culture in Crisis*
by J.D. Vance

*How Washington Really Works*
by Charles Peters

*Lincoln: Team of Rivals*
by Doris Kearns Goodwin

*Nature Writings* by John Muir

*A People's History of the United States*
by Howard Zinn

*Profiles in Courage*
by John F. Kennedy

*White Trash: The 400-Year Untold
History of Class in America*
by Nancy Isenberg

# Resources

## A SHORT LIST OF ORGANIZATIONS *THAT SUPPORT WOMEN*

> *Girls Incorporated:* Dedicated to inspiring all girls to be strong, smart, and bold. With roots dating to 1864, Girls Inc. has provided educational programs to millions of American girls, particularly those in high-risk, underserved areas.

> *League of Women Voters:* Fighting since 1920 to improve systems of government and impact public policies through citizen education and advocacy. The LWV is a grassroots organization that operates at the national, state, and local levels.

> *NARAL:* NARAL Pro-Choice America engages in political action and efforts to oppose restrictions on abortion and expand access to abortion.

> *NOW:* Founded in 1966, the National Organization for Women works to bring about equality for all women.

> *Planned Parenthood:* More than 100 years old, PP delivers vital reproductive health care, sex education, and information to millions of women, men, and young people worldwide.

> *She Should Run:* Focused on expanding the talent pool of future elected female leaders. She Should Run started as a project in 2008 and has evolved to become a movement working to inspire women and girls to aspire towards public leadership.

> *Step Up for Women:* Engages professional women to inspire teen girls through after-school and mentorship programs.

> *The Global Women's Project:* An Australia-based non-profit organization that supports grassroots women's organizations in developing and disadvantaged communities to provide opportunities for women.

> *Women for Women:* In countries affected by conflict and war, Women for Women International supports marginalized women to earn and save money, improve health and well-being, influence decisions in their home and community, and connect to networks for support.

> *YWCA:* Counts more than 25 million members in 106 countries, including 2.6 million across the U.S. The YWCA's mission is to eliminate racism and empower women.

## WAYS TO GET INVOLVED *IN YOUR COMMUNITY*

> Participate and volunteer for your community's annual events, such as an art fair or 5K

> Join a local Indivisible group

> Volunteer at a soup kitchen or domestic violence shelter

> Become a Big Sister

> Join the PTA or volunteer at your child's school

> Become a board member of a non-profit organization

> Attend town halls and city council meetings

> Write letters and make phone calls to your elected officials

> Run for office, be it the school board, city council, or a state or national position

> Become an active congregant in a place of worship

## CONSIDERING RUNNING FOR OFFICE? *CHECK THESE RESOURCES*

*sheshouldrun.org*

*runforsomething.net*

*emilyslist.org*

*howtorunforoffice.org*

 # Photo Credits

# Text Credits

## Family Matters

12  Prevention.com, November 3, 2011.

15  Remarks in conversation with Oprah Winfrey at the United State of Women Summit, June 14, 2016.

16  *New York Times*, October 28, 2008.

17  Brattleboro *Reformer*, December 6, 2007.

18  Speech to Democratic National Convention, 2016.

21  Remarks by the First Lady, Nick Cannon, and Seth Meyers in a discussion with Howard University students, September 1, 2016.

22  Speech to Democratic National Convention, 2008.

23  Remarks to students at Elizabeth Garrett Anderson School, April 2009.

## Good Relations

26  *Good Housekeeping*, November 2008.

27  *O, The Oprah Magazine*, November 2007.

28  *Chicago Tribune*, April 22, 2007.

29  Speech to Democratic National Convention, 2012.

31  Joslyn Pine, *Wit and Wisdom of America's First Ladies: A Book of Quotations*, (Mineola: Dover Publications, 2014).

32  Remarks in conversation with Oprah Winfrey at the United State of Women Summit, June 14, 2016.

34  Peter Slevin, *Michelle Obama: A Life* (New York: Vintage Books, 2016), 130–131.

34  Remarks at *Glamour's* "The Power of the Educated Girl" panel, September 29, 2015.

35  Remarks at *Glamour's* "The Power of the Educated Girl" panel, September 29, 2015.

37  Remarks at the Summit of the Mandela Washington Fellowship for Young African Leaders, July 30, 2014.

## Working Woman

41  Remarks in conversation with Oprah Winfrey at the United State of Women Summit, June 14, 2016.

42  Remarks in conversation with Oprah Winfrey at the United State of Women Summit, June 14, 2016.

43  *Vogue*, September 2007.

44  Remarks in conversation with Oprah Winfrey at the United State of Women Summit, June 14, 2016.

46  Remarks in conversation with Oprah Winfrey at the United State of Women Summit, June 14, 2016.

48  Remarks to students at Elizabeth Garrett Anderson School, April 2, 2009.

49  Peter Slevin, *Michelle Obama: A Life* (New York: Vintage Books, 2016), 80.

50  *Essence*, September 2007.

51  Remarks in conversation with Oprah Winfrey at the United State of Women Summit, June 14, 2016.

## Style + Substance

54  Kate Betts, *Everyday Icon: Michelle Obama and the Power of Style* (New York: Potter Style, 2011), 10.

55  Peter Slevin, *Michelle Obama: A Life* (New York: Vintage Books, 2016), 4.

58  *Vogue*, December 2016.

59  *The Telegraph*, July 26, 2008.

61  *Vogue*, March 2009.

62  In *Ebony*, as reported in Kate Betts, *Everyday Icon: Michelle Obama and the Power of Style* (New York: Potter Style, 2011), 126.

63  *The View*, June 18, 2008.

64  *The View*, June 18, 2008.

65  *The Tonight Show with Jay Leno*, October 27, 2008.

## Strength in the Face of Adversity

69  Prevention.com, November 3, 2011.

70  Remarks at Manchester Clinton/Kaine campaign rally, October 13, 2016.

72  Last speech as First Lady to honor 2017 school counselor of the year, January 3, 2017.

73  Remarks in conversation with Oprah Winfrey at the United State of Women Summit, June 14, 2016.

74  Peter Slevin, *Michelle Obama: A Life* (New York: Vintage Books, 2016), 132–133.

75  Speech to Democratic National Convention, 2016.

76  Remarks in conversation with Oprah Winfrey at the United State of Women Summit, June 14, 2016.

76  *Essence*, September 2008.

77  Kate Betts, *Everyday Icon: Michelle Obama and the Power of Style* (New York: Potter Style, 2011), 113.

78  Remarks in conversation with Oprah Winfrey at the United State of Women Summit, June 14, 2016.